Thailand Tourism

NOTES FOR PROFESSIONAL LIBRARIANS AND LIBRARY USERS

This is an original book title published by The Haworth Hospitality & Tourism Press™, an imprint of The Haworth Press, Inc. Unless otherwise noted in specific chapters with attribution, materials in this book have not been previously published elsewhere in any format or language.

CONSERVATION AND PRESERVATION NOTES

All books published by The Haworth Press, Inc., and its imprints are printed on certified pH neutral, acid-free book grade paper. This paper meets the minimum requirements of American National Standard for Information Sciences-Permanence of Paper for Printed Material, ANSI Z39.48-1984.

DIGITAL OBJECT IDENTIFIER (DOI) LINKING

The Haworth Press is participating in reference linking for elements of our original books. (For more information on reference linking initiatives, please consult the CrossRef Web site at www.crossref.org.) When citing an element of this book such as a chapter, include the element's Digital Object Identifier (DOI) as the last item of the reference. A Digital Object Identifier is a persistent, authoritative, and unique identifier that a publisher assigns to each element of a book. Because of its persistence, DOIs will enable The Haworth Press and other publishers to link to the element referenced, and the link will not break over time. This will be a great resource in scholarly research.

Thailand Tourism

Arthur Asa Berger

Routledge
Taylor & Francis Group
New York London

First published 2007 by
The Haworth Hospitality & Tourism Press™

Published 2013 by Routledge
52 Vanderbilt Avenue, New York, NY 10017
2 Park Square, Milton Park, Abingdon, Oxon OX14 4RN

Routledge is an imprint of the Taylor & Francis Group, an informa business

PUBLISHER'S NOTE

The development, preparation, and publication of this work has been undertaken with great care. However, the Publisher, employees, editors, and agents of The Haworth Press are not responsible for any errors contained herein or for consequences that may ensue from use of materials or information contained in this work. The Haworth Press is committed to the dissemination of ideas and information according to the highest standards of intellectual freedom and the free exchange of ideas. Statements made and opinions expressed in this publication do not necessarily reflect the views of the Publisher, Directors, management, or staff of The Haworth Press, Inc., or an endorsement by them.

Cover design by Marylouise E. Doyle.

Library of Congress Cataloging-in-Publication Data

Berger, Arthur Asa, 1933-
  Thailand tourism / Arthur Asa Berger.
    p. cm.
  Includes bibliographical references and indexes.
  1. Thailand—Description and travel. 2. Thailand—Civilization. 3. Tourism—Thailand. I. Title.

DS566.2.B47 2007
338.4'791593—dc22

                                                                    2006022963

ISBN 13: 978-0-789-03184-6 (pbk)
ISBN 13: 978-0-789-03183-9 (hbk)

CONTENTS

PART III: THAILAND ON MY MIND

ABOUT THE AUTHOR

Arthur Asa Berger, PhD, is professor emeritus of Broadcast and Electronic Communication Art at San Francisco State University, where he taught between 1965 and 2003. Shortly after receiving his MA degree in journalism and creative writing from the University of Iowa in 1956, he was drafted and served in the US Army in the Military District of Washington in Washington, DC, where he was a feature writer and speech writer in the District's Public Information Office. After he got out of the Army, he spent a year touring Europe and then went on to the University of Minnesota for his PhD.

Dr. Berger is the author of numerous articles, book reviews, and more than 50 books on the mass media, popular culture, humor, tourism, and everyday life. His books include *Ocean Travel and Cruising, Vietnam Tourism, Deconstructing Travel,* and *Media and Communication Research Methods*. He is also author of several darkly comic academic mysteries, such as *Postmortem for a Postmodernist, The Hamlet Case, Mistake in Identity*, and *The Mass Comm Murders*. He lives in Mill Valley, California.

Foreword

It is my pleasure and honor to write the foreword for this book, *Thailand Tourism,* by Arthur Asa Berger. Through this book, readers will discover not only the uniqueness of Thai culture, traditions, beliefs, arts, heritage sites, and language, but they will also gain an understanding of the nature of the Thai people.

The analytical information on Thai society and culture presented in this book will help those who are interested in Thailand, especially the Westerners who are not accustomed to Eastern culture, to absorb and recognize various facets of the Thai culture, such as the *wai*—the act of greeting and paying respect. This book also familiarizes the readers with Thai cuisine and its various dishes, which are world-renowned for their characteristic flavors. The "signs and symbols" of Thailand depicted in this book provide a panoramic insight into the rich and ancient heritage embedded in modern-day Thai lifestyle, which is reflected in the "two skylines of Thailand" as described by Professor Berger.

As a Thai, I appreciate Professor Berger's brilliant effort to illustrate the charm and amazing aspects of my beloved country Thailand.

Dr. Darunee Hirunruk
Dean, School of Communication Arts
University of the Thai Chamber of Commerce

Thailand Tourism
© 2007 by The Haworth Press, Inc. All rights reserved.
doi:10.1300/5789_a

ix

When the rest of the world discovered that a country existed whose men and women were mainly concerned with dedicating themselves to life's refined pleasures and arts, the news created a gust that blew through the world of tourism, carrying millions of admirers with it in numbers that have grown from year to year.

Not only does Thailand feed many nations with the bounty of its rice fields, but it also teaches them how to transform a basic human need, that of securing a daily minimum of calories, into a perennial feast. We all have lessons to learn from the Thais. Who else on this planet could have deterred the world powers from colonizing them, by showing (among other means) charming smiles and handsome diplomacy. And, at the same time, managed to integrate most of the modern benefits of the West.

A nation that embraces gastronomy and love can't be wrong by any judgment.

Andre Gayot, *Gault Millau:*
The Best of Thailand, 1991: 2

Thailand should satisfy just about any traveler's hunger for the exotic, the beautiful, the thrillingly different. But it is a country whose very lure for the foreigner threatens to make it a parody of itself.

It is a country with a deep respect for family and monarchy, and a country with a huge prostitution industry and a corrupt military. It is a thriving place for business, but has serious problems with international copyright and trademark policy. It is a physically lovely country that is, like many others, being degraded by logging, wildlife exploitation, and overdevelopment. It is a microcosm of all that is right and wrong with tourism, and the traveler's special role as pilgrim, adventurer, and consumer.

James O'Reilly and Larry Habegger,
Travelers' Tales Thailand, 2002: xix

Preface

Why do people travel? And how do they make up their minds about where to go when they decide to travel? In particular, what makes people decide to visit Thailand rather than some other country? This book, devoted to an analysis of tourism in Thailand, must answer these questions. Tourism is now the largest industry in the world. Something is leading millions and millions of people to decide to become tourists and see some part of the world that, for one reason or another, attracts them.

WHY PEOPLE TRAVEL

In recent decades, people seem to have moved away from spending money mainly on material goods and possessions to spending money on experiences they believe will enrich their lives, and it is tourism to foreign lands that has become a major beneficiary of this shift. Whatever it is that explains why people travel, it becomes a very powerful part of many people's lives—a passion of sorts. That may help explain why, in the course of my travels, I have met a considerable number of people who have confided to me, without much of a sense of guilt, that "we're spending our children's legacy." Travel, for some people, changes from becoming a way of amusing oneself and satisfying one's curiosity to a need, to something that shapes their lives.

THE OBLIGATION TO TRAVEL

There may be an element of hedonism and even selfishness, to varying degrees, involved in tourism—or the behavior of some tourists, to be more accurate. But the most powerful impetus to tourism is a desire to see the world, to know more about its people, and to have life-affirming, life-enhancing experiences.

Psychologists tell us that it is important for our mental well-being and health to get away from our normal routines and take vacations, so there are physical and psychological benefits to tourism. Some culture critics argue that mass tourism is now one more product of our capitalist economic system and that people find themselves obliged, one might say, to travel. That is, there is an element of compulsion to travel that many people feel. They need to feel "world class." The puritan ethic of hard work and thrift has been replaced by the consumption ethic and people now feel forced to entertain themselves, have fun, and, more directly for our purposes, become tourists.

Jean Baudrillard has explained this phenomenon in his book *The Consumer Society: Myths and Structures.* He writes:

> There is no question for the consumer, for the modern citizen, of evading this enforced happiness and enjoyment, which is the equivalent in the new ethics of the traditional imperative to labour and produce. Modern man spends less and less of his life in production within work and more and more of it in the *production* and continual innovation of his own needs and well-being. He must constantly see to it that all his potentialities, all his consumer capacities are mobilized. If he forgets to do so, he will be gently and insistently reminded that he has no right not to be happy. It is not, then, true that he is passive. He is engaged in—has to engage in—continual activity. . . . Hence the revival of a *universal curiosity.* . . . You have to try *everything,* for consumerist man is haunted by the fear of "missing" something, some form of enjoyment. You never know whether a particular encounter, a particular experience (Christmas in the Canaries, eel in whiskey, the Prado, LSD, Japanese-style love-making) will not elicit some "sensation." It is no longer desire, or even "taste," or a specific inclination that are at stake, but a generalized curiosity, driven by a vague sense of unease—it is the "fun morality" or the imperative to enjoy oneself, to exploit to the full one's potential for thrills, pleasure or gratification. (1998: 80)

In Baudrillard's analysis, there is a good deal of travel and tourism involved—as people seeking sensations have to decide whether to visit the Canary Islands, the Prado in Madrid, or Japan for "real" Japanese-style lovemaking, among other things they might be considering.

In a sense, then, according to Baudrillard, tourism is one more burden people must bear in meeting their need to experience life to the fullest. And if Japanese-style lovemaking doesn't seem interesting, there is always lovemaking in Thailand to consider, where it will be a lot less expensive and, perhaps, even more exotic.

WHY THAILAND?

Once people have decided to take a trip somewhere—that is, to become travelers and tourists—the question of where to go arises. People who do a good deal of traveling generally find themselves literally bombarded with catalogs from tourist companies and travel agencies and e-mail messages about cruises and special deals on tourist packages to here and there. There are also advertisements in magazines and newspapers about different and interesting-looking destinations.

So there's tremendous choice that people face when they decide to travel. Should they take another cruise? Should they go back to Paris or, perhaps, see what Bulgaria is like. Why they choose Thailand— from all the other possibilities open to them—is the subject of this book. It has to do, in large part, with images people have of Thailand as an exotic but safe place to visit. They may have seen a film with Leonardo di Caprio in *The Beach* (2000), or a television show about Thailand or read an article about Thailand in some newspaper or magazine. In the popular imagination, I would suggest, there is a very strong connection between Thailand and sexuality, so we may think of Thailand as symbolizing what might be called "the exotic– erotic" for many tourists contemplating a trip to Thailand. Despite the horrible tsunamis that ravaged Phuket and many other resort areas, Thailand remains a major destination for millions of people and the number of tourists visiting Thailand in 2006 was not expected to diminish greatly because of the earthquake in Sumatra and resultant tsunamis.

GETTING TO THAILAND
FROM THE UNITED STATES

Going to Thailand from America takes a good deal of time and effort. From San Francisco, some package tour companies estimate it will take approximately twenty hours to fly to Thailand, and one loses a day, as well. Tourists from the East Coast have to spend another six hours flying to San Francisco, so a trip to Thailand is somewhat of an ordeal. (Of course, travel to any Southeast Asian country takes approximately the same amount of time.) That's why most tours to Thailand for Americans start on the third day—assuming the tourist has arrived the day before, on the second day and spent it resting and perhaps walking around Bangkok a bit. And most of the last day is usually lost, as well—devoted to delivering tourists to Bangkok. The next morning they will be taken to the airport in Bangkok for their return flight. Thus, a tour of Thailand that is advertised for sixteen days involves thirteen nights at hotels.

To set the stage for this analysis of Thailand as a tourist destination, I begin this book with a discussion of the tourism industry in general. I define tourism (there is some debate about how to define tourists and whether it is possible to differentiate them from travelers) and offer some statistics about tourism in various countries, including Thailand—and Asian countries competing with Thailand for tourists. There is a great deal of competition for tourists—among countries and among different regions in countries and among cities in a given region—because of the economic benefits of tourism. It is estimated that tourism represents 6 percent of Thailand's gross domestic product and is the largest industry in the country.

A NOTE ON METHODOLOGY

Tourism is a subject that covers a number of different areas of life and, accordingly, I have used several methodologies in this analysis of tourism in Thailand. This book offers some statistics on tourism, in general, and tourism in Thailand, in particular, and in that respect it is, broadly speaking sociological. It also is anthropological in that it has a good deal to say about Thai culture, which I suggest, is one of

Thailand's main attractions. And this book is ethnological in that it relies on my experiences and interpretations of various aspects of Thai culture based on my travel there. Finally, it is semiotic in that it sees Thailand as a vast sign system whose most important signs I analyze and interpret. My approach is probably best described as an example of cultural studies, which uses a number of different disciplines to deal with tourism in Thailand (and any subject to which it is applied).

Tourists who visit Thailand invariably take photographs of the main sights and sites—famous temples, Buddha statues, *wats* (temples), Buddhist monks, paradisical beaches, important buildings, historic ruins, and so on. These are the signs that capture Thailand for them and it is the more important Thai signs—defining the term broadly—that I interpret.

I became interested in using semiotics as a means of analyzing countries after reading *Empire of Signs* by Roland Barthes, a study of important Japanese signs. In this book he writes that he cannot capture all of Japan but he can deal with some of its more revealing signs. I used this methodology in my book *Vietnam Tourism* and employ it in this book as well. When you are "a stranger in a strange land," you see things that the natives often pay little attention to, and I hope this analysis will reveal interesting things about Thailand and help explain why it remains such a fascinating, beguiling, and wonderful country to visit.

Acknowledgments

I would like to thank Kaye Chon for suggesting I write this book and the various editors, copy editors, production editors, and marketing people at The Haworth Press for their assistance with this book. I also want to thank Professor Ross Dowling for helping me connect with two Thai informants, his doctoral students Sujittra Inthrarat and Attama Boonpalit. Sujittra Inthrarat sent a suggested itinerary in Thailand, which I have reproduced in this book. And Attama Boonpalit has sent me numerous long and very detailed and informative e-mail messages about contemporary Thai culture, provided me with very important insights, and helped me escape from making a number of errors.

I also owe a debt of gratitude to all the scholars and writers who have written about tourism, travel, Buddhism, and Thai culture and society, for helping me connect the "flashes" and insights I had when I visited Thailand with analyses that were helpful to me in explaining and analyzing these "flashes" in more depth.

Thailand Tourism
© 2007 by The Haworth Press, Inc. All rights reserved.
doi:10.1300/5789_c   *xix*

PART I:
TOURISM IN THAILAND

Thailand, or Siam as it was called until the 1940s, has never been colonized by a foreign power, while all of its South-East Asian neighbors have undergone European imperialism (or more recently ideological domination by Communism—which originated in Europe) at one time or another. True, it has suffered periodic invasions on the part of the Burmese and the Khmers and was briefly occupied by the Japanese in WWII, but the kingdom was never externally controlled long enough to dampen the Thais' serious individualism. I say serious because the Thais are so often depicted as fun-loving, happy-go-lucky folk (which they often are), but this quality is something they have worked hard to preserve.

This is not to say that Thailand has not experienced any western influence. Like other Asian countries it has both suffered and benefited from contact with foreign cultures. But the ever-changing spirit of Thai culture has remained dominant, even in modern city life. The end result is that Thailand has much to interest the traveler: historic culture, lively arts, exotic islands, nightlife, a tradition of friendliness and hospitality to strangers, and one of the world's most exciting cuisines.

Cummings, *Thailand,* 1990: 7

Everyone knows something about Thailand. The country is known to many as the home of a wonderful cuisine, great package tours, child prostitution, fabulous silk, fake Rolex Watches and magnificent temples. We learn about the country through tourist advertising, business and educational exchanges, films and news reports; these fragments reinforce the country's seductive appeal. For Thailand does not permit distancing but rather sucks us into a sensual world of exotic sights, sounds, tastes and smells.

Van Esterick, *Materializing Thailand,* 2002: 3

Chapter 1

Tourism, Travelers, and Thailand

Tourism is now considered to be the largest industry in the world, having supplanted the oil industry a number of years ago. The World Travel and Tourism Council estimates that by 2010 tourism and travel will be an 8 trillion dollar a year industry employing approximately 330 million people. In 1998 global tourism was a 3.6-trillion-dollar-a-year industry, employing more than 230 million people; so projections for the growth of the tourism industry are very optimistic. There are approximately 6 billion people in the world; so an industry that employs 230 million people is employing 1 out of every 24 people, but, in actuality, tourism employs a higher percentage of those who are of working age.

It is, then, an important factor in the development of modern consumer cultures, ones in which leisure activities like tourism are becoming increasingly important. Tourism is a way of combining things like air travel, hotel stays, restaurant dining, museum visits, and other cultural activities all in one package. The term "package tour" is, then, very accurate. Tourism, Baudrillard suggests, must be seen as part of the postmodern imperative of continual consumption in order to live to the fullest and to have an exciting narrative thrust to one's life.

There is some disagreement among scholars about how to define tourism and whether it is possible to differentiate it from travel. I discuss these matters before offering some more detailed statistics on the tourism industry.

Thailand Tourism
© 2007 by The Haworth Press, Inc. All rights reserved.
doi:10.1300/5789_01

DEFINITIONS OF TOURISM

I start with the definition offered by the World Tourism Organization (2002a):

> It comprises the activities of persons traveling to and staying in places outside their usual environment for not more than one consecutive year for leisure, business and other purposes not related to the exercise of an activity remunerated from within the place visited.

The root of the term "tourist" is the Greek word *tornos,* which is a simple tool that was used for making a circle. So there is, built into the term tourism, the notion that a tour involves traveling in a circle, of leaving from a particular place and returning there at the end of one's travel. In the travel industry, tours are understood to be, generally speaking, a group form of travel in which the route is specific, there is a certain amount of regimentation involved, and eventually the tourists return to where they started.

In his book *The Tourist: A New Theory of the Leisure Class* Dean MacCannell defines the tourist in the following manner:

> "Tourist" is used to mean two things in this book. It designates actual tourists: sightseers, mainly middle-class, who are at this moment deployed through the entire world in search of experience. I want the book to serve as a sociological study of this group. But I should make it known that, from the beginning, I intended something more. The tourist is an actual person, or real people are actually tourists. At the same time, "the tourist" is one of the best models for modern-man-in-general. I am equally interested in "the tourist" in this second, metasociological sense of the term. Our first apprehension of modern civilization, it seems to me, emerges in the mind of the tourist. (1976: 1)

MacCannell sees tourists as models for modern man. His definition suggests that to be a human being, or, at least, a modern man (and woman) nowadays, is to be a tourist. Tourism, then, becomes modern man's and woman's primary occupation and preoccupation, their most important means of self-definition.

Michel de Certeau, in his book *The Practice of Everyday Life,* has suggested that all novels involve travel, as characters move from one place to another. He writes:

> Narrative structures have the status of spatial syntaxes. By means of a whole panoply of codes, ordered ways of proceeding and constraints, they regulate changes in space (or moves from one place to another) made by stories in the form of places put in linear of interlaced series: from here (Paris) one goes there (Montargis) . . . Every story is a travel story—a spatial practice. (1984: 115)

What he writes about narratives, such as short stories and novels, it sounds, curiously, very much like a package tour.

If that is the case, and all stories involve travel, its opposite suggests that *travel is a form of novelization or memoir-ization of our lives.* If we think of our lives as narratives, much of the excitement we experience comes from our travels and adventures, and our everyday lives become a kind of rather monotonous, eventless, uninteresting filler between our travels. That may be one reason why tourism and travel become so important in many people's lives.

The Internet encyclopedia, Wikipedia, offers the following insights into tourism (slightly edited for readability):

> Tourism can be defined as the act of travel for the purpose of recreation, and the provision of services for this act. A "tourist" is someone who travels at least fifty miles from home, as defined by the World Tourism Organization, a United Nations body. A more comprehensive definition would be that tourism is a service industry, comprising a number of tangible and intangible components. The tangible elements include transportation systems—air, rail, road, water and now, space; hospitality services—accommodation, foods and beverages, tours, souvenirs; and related services such as banking, insurance and safety & security. The intangible elements include: rest and relaxation, culture, escape, adventure, new and different experiences. (www .wikipedia.org., 2004)

The discussion of tourism in this Internet encyclopedia article adds that many countries depend, to a considerable amount, on tourism and the money spent by tourists, and thus countries encourage tourism through nongovernmental and governmental agencies. The article contrasts "tourism" and "travel," suggesting that the latter term implies a "more purposeful journey." It points out that the term "tourism" often suggests shallowness and superficiality.

I take issue with this description of tourism as necessarily superficial and trivial, even though some package tours are very fast moving ("If it's Tuesday, we must be in Madrid") and don't allow time for so-called in-depth experiences. We often use the term "travel" in connection with business, but that oversimplifies things. Does a business traveler, who spends some time visiting a cathedral or museum in some foreign land where he or she has been sent on a business trip, become a tourist? And if a tourist happens to do some business while on a tour, does he or she become a traveler?

I would suggest that we use the terms interchangeably. After all, tourists have to travel—using automobiles, trains, planes, and ships—to the places they visit and travelers often do things that tourists do, so it doesn't make that much sense to differentiate the terms—except, perhaps, at the furthest edge of the travel/tourism continuum. Tourism is done for pleasure and diversion but it is also, as anyone who has done any traveling can testify, very hard work, often involving long flights and endless hassles at airports, screwups at hotels, and mix-ups of one kind or another, among other things.

Tourism also has an element of risk and danger to it, as the tsunami disaster of December 26, 2004, shows. As a result of the earthquake and tsunamis of that date, thousands of tourists, from all over the world, were killed in Phuket, Thailand, and other beach resorts in Thailand and in other parts of Asia. There is reason to believe that many of the tourists in Phuket and other resorts in Thailand could have been saved if the Thai meteorological service had issued warnings immediately after it found out about the underwater earthquake. It decided not to do so lest it disturb tourists there and damage the tourism industry (see Exhibit 1.1).

EXHIBIT 1.1. A report on the tsunami of December 26, 2004

"Thai weather officials under attack for lack of warning"

Thailand's meteorological department knew by 8:10 am (local time) on Sunday—about an hour before the first waves hit—that a powerful earthquake had struck near Sumatra, and they discussed the possibility that the quake could cause large sea disturbances. . . . But without definitive proof of an imminent tsunami, the meteorological department dared not issue a national warning lest it be accused of spreading panic and hurting the tourism industry if the disturbances did not materialize.

"Not every earthquake that occurs in the sea will cause a tsunami; it is very difficult to know," said Sumalee Prachuab, a seismologist at the department. "If we issue a warning about the possibility of a tsunami, people will panic very much."

"Phuket is for the tourists, and [if we warn] they will cancel everything," she said. "Then if the tsunami did not occur, the meteorological department will have many telephone calls complaining "why did you make that prediction?"

Source: Amy Kazmin, Financial Times, December 30, 2004: 2.

TOURISM AS ADVENTURE

Tourism is, by its nature, a kind of adventure, and there is actually a category of tourism called "Adventure Travel," and a subcategory of it called "Soft Adventure Travel." Many travelers think of themselves as being adventurers and being different from people who do not travel very much and who to some extent, as Thoreau put it, "lead lives of quiet desperation." But what is an adventure?

Georg Simmel, a German sociologist, described adventures as follows:

The most general form of adventure is its dropping out of the continuity of life. "Wholeness of life," after all, refers to the fact that a consistent process runs through the individual components of life, however crassly and irreconcilably distinct they may be. What we call an adventure stands in contrast to that interlocking of life-links, to that feeling that those counter-currents, turnings, and knots still, after all, spin forth a continuous thread. . . .We ascribe to the adventure a beginning and an end much sharper than those to be discovered in the other forms of our experience. The adventure is freed of the entanglements and concatenations which are characteristic of those forms and is given a meaning in and of itself. (Quoted in Frisby and Featherstone, 1997: 222)

Thus, we can distinguish between our everyday lives, in which we follow routines and which have no beginnings and endings of consequence. Everything continues in everyday life. But in an adventure, there is a distinct beginning and ending to the adventure and it is a qualitatively different kind of experience for us.

Henri Lefebvre, a French sociologist, has described everyday life in his book *Everyday Life in the Modern World* as "made of recurrences: gestures of labour and leisure, mechanical movements both human and properly mechanic, hours, days, weeks, months, year, liner and cyclical repetitions" (1971: 18). Everyday life, or the quotidian, as he sometimes describes it, involves phenomena that we all take for granted, that which is undated and seemingly insignificant. In his book he discusses ideological matters connected to everyday life, which are not of any concern to us here. What is important is that our lives are immersed in everyday life's routines and recurrences, and what travel does is allow us to escape from everyday life, if only for a short period of time. But this time is enough to recharge our batteries, which is why psychologists now advise people to take vacations.

Adventures are very similar, Simmel suggests, to works of art, which also have strongly delineated beginnings and endings that serve to detach these works from the seamless, endless continuity of everyday life. Thus, the adventurer is the person who lives in the present, Simmel argues, and the same applies to tourists—who, while they are traveling, find themselves detached from their everyday lives and their concerns and focus their attention on the activities of the moment in which they are involved. One of the things that makes travel so memorable for people is that they can escape, for a certain amount of time, from their everyday lives and routines.

As I pointed out earlier, Michel de Certeau has written that every story is a travel story. I have suggested that if this is correct, then all travel can be seen as a kind of story in which we write our lives in terms of the adventures we experience. Simmel's notions about the bounded quality of adventures and works of art helps explain why our travels are adventures and similar in nature to works of art in which we help make our lives, if only for a while, similar to the stories we find in works of literary art.

KINDS OF TOURISM

Tourists travel for a variety of different reasons. Let me list and briefly describe some of the more common kinds of tourism. I should point out that these kinds of travel are not mutually exclusive and tourists often combine a number of them in a trip.

Adventure Tourism

These tourists are searching for adventures in climbing mountains, kayaking, trekking for long periods of time, and visiting places off the beaten track as far as traditional tourism is concerned. A diluted form of adventure tourism called "soft adventure tourism" exists for people who want to rough it to some degree but not to the extent of regular adventure tourists; they want to be able to spend time in important cities and at beautiful beaches. Bird watchers go all over the world searching for birds, which I would include as a soft-adventure kind of tourism.

Cultural Tourism

These tourists are interested in investigating the cultures of the places they visit and tend to focus on cities where there are important cathedrals, temples, museums, symphony halls, opera houses, and other places of a similar nature.

Disaster Tourism

Some tourists like to go to the sites of disasters, of one kind or another, to see for themselves what happened and, I would suggest, to "participate in history" by doing so. Thus, after the disastrous tsunami of December 2004, some tourists booked flights to places that suffered from the tsunamis.

Drug Tourism

These tourists visit places where they will have easy access to drugs that are difficult to obtain in their native lands.

Ecotourism

Ecotourists go to places where attention is paid to ecological matters, such as rain forests, to help preserve them. Many cities and regions that are of interest to tourists have jumped on the ecology bandwagon, so to speak, and work hard to maintain their sites in an ecologically correct manner. Ecotourists have had a positive impact upon the tourism industry, though there is some question about whether, despite their best intentions, they actually end up damaging some of the fragile places they visit.

Family Tourism

These tourists travel for family get-togethers: graduations, weddings, births, bar mitzvahs, funerals, and other important events in the life cycle.

Food Tourism

This kind of tourism is of special interest to "foodies," people whose interest in cooking and passion for foreign cuisines form the basis of their tourism and many tourist agencies now offer tours based on gastronomy.

Medical Tourism

Medical tourists are people who spend time in countries where they can have medical procedures done relatively inexpensively or have access to medical practices not allowed in their native countries. In Thailand, for example, many international tourists come to have plastic surgery done, because of the high quality and bargain prices of the plastic surgery industry there. A weaker version of medical tourism involves people who go to spas or other places of a similar nature.

Sex Tourism

Sex tourism is, unfortunately, a major component of the tourism industry in many countries and Thailand is rather notorious for its highly developed sex tourism. Sex tourists visit countries where there will be relatively easy access to the kind of sexual partners they desire. This runs the gamut from heterosexual sex (and, in certain cases, with sex tourism expatriates who are sometimes called "sexpatriates") to gay sex and pedophilia.

Sports Tourism

Many tourists go to other countries to do things such as skiing, cycling, kayaking, and playing golf, or attending games involving sports teams that they may follow.

* * *

We should recognize that tourists generally have many different reasons for traveling and not just one. Someone may go to a different city or a different country to attend a wedding, but might also visit museums and temples or attend musical and dance performances during that visit. They might even take an extended tour of the region or country after the event they came for has concluded.

Cities, where tourism is a major industry, have an interest in making sure that they cater to the varied interests of the tourists who visit them. Thus, for example, San Francisco, a city of only 700,000 people, has a symphony orchestra, an opera, a number of museums, professional baseball, basketball, and football teams, many excellent restaurants, and is close to sites of natural beauty such as Muir Woods and the wine country.

In the course of a lifetime of being a tourist, a person might become many different kinds of tourist. In my younger days I was a backpacker and adventure tourist but as I have grown older, I have mellowed into a soft-adventure tourist and a cultural tourist. There is, as my list of the different kinds of tourists suggests, a great deal of segmentation in the travel and tourism industry.

USES AND GRATIFICATIONS OF TOURISM

A number of years ago, some social scientists involved with mass mediated communications started focusing their attention on the uses people made of the television shows they watched and radio programs they listened to, and the gratifications the media provided for its audiences. The social scientists learned about these various uses and gratifications by asking people why they watched the television shows they watched or listened to certain kinds of radio shows. This approach involved a change from studying effects media had on people to the way they used the media. In a book I wrote on media studies, *Media Analysis Techniques,* I listed a number of the more important uses and gratifications that scholars developed, which I will adapt for understanding tourism in Thailand.

1. To experience beauty. One of Thailand's main selling points as a tourist destination is that it is a beautiful country, with gorgeous islands and pristine paradisical beaches and other spectacular natural areas.
2. To satisfy curiosity and gain information about the world. Tourists choose to visit countries because they think they will be interesting and will offer the chance to experience and learn about a different culture. Thailand is generally thought of as "exotic" and thus a country that will provide new sensations to people and give them new insights into the human condition.
3. To obtain a sense of fellowship with others. Travel literature describes the Thai people as warm and friendly and this sense that tourists will be well received and can get to know some Thais is a strong motivation.
4. To obtain outlets for sexual drives in a guilt-free manner. Thailand is a country where there is easy access to sex, of all kinds, and where the people do not have the same repressed attitudes toward sex that you find in many countries. For better or worse, Thailand has become a "sex magnet" and this, among other things, appeals to many tourists—especially those from coun-

tries where there is a certain amount of sexual repression. It is commonplace that when tourists travel to foreign countries, they are willing to do things they would never do at home, and this includes sexual behavior.

5. To reinforce national identity. One thing travel does is make us think about how different our way of life is from the countries we visit, and in countries like Thailand, where the differences with countries in the West are profound, we are able to see what's distinctive about our culture in very sharp detail. In extreme cases, this phenomenon is called "culture shock."

6. To be amused and entertained. Thailand, with its exotic (to Western people) culture, also provides unusual kinds of entertainments—such as kickboxing, classical dance, and music, and a very distinctive cuisine. There is a search for novelty, then, involved in tourism.

We can see, then, that Thailand has a number of distinctive characteristics that it uses to sell itself to tourists considering a visit there. It is its "otherness" as an exotic-erotic destination that is a powerful lure for people, especially those in the West. I will return to this matter of Thailand's "otherness" later, when I compare Thai culture with American culture.

TOURISM AND THE LIBIDO

Many scholars writing about tourism discuss the matter of the tourists' search for authenticity and for "otherness." This notion of "otherness" refers to the desire to have different experiences from those that people have in their everyday lives in their native countries. But the search for novelty is, I would suggest, connected to other forces in the psyche. Freud has written that "in the adult, novelty always constitutes the condition of orgasm" (Barthes, 1975: 41).

What Freud's statement suggests is that there is actually a sexual dimension to the search for novelty and that finding novelty, which is one of the main purposes of tourism, has a libidinal payoff, so to speak. Visiting foreign (and, therefore, new) countries is, in a way, similar to getting to know someone new and exploring that new sexual partner's body. All of this is connected to our unconscious—

a realm of our psyches that is not accessible to us, generally speaking. And most tourists, if asked whether they thought there was a subliminal sexual aspect to travel in new countries, would find the idea amusing and possibly absurd. They might say that travel in Thailand has an overtly sexual aspect to it, and in that many tourists to Thailand go there seeking sexual partners. But the idea that tourism and travel in new places is sexual in nature seems, on the surface, far-fetched.

But is not it possible that compulsive travelers have something of the Don Juan about them, and that the experience of being in new countries has a kind of thrill that has something of the orgasmic about it? That may help explain why some people find themselves needing to visit new places all the time and why their travels often lead to heightened moments of bliss—not far removed from actually having orgasms. Thus, traveling to a new country is quite close to anticipating having sex and, in a way, it is having sex, but of a different nature from physical sex between two partners.

PEOPLE ON THE MOVE: STATISTICS ON TOURISM IN EUROPE AND ASIA

According to the World Tourism Organization (2004) there were 526 million international tourist arrivals between January and August of 2004. That works out, if we add another four months to the number, to approximately 785 million international tourist arrivals during the year. That means there were an enormous number of people "on the move," going here and there for various reasons—approximately one out of seven people on the earth was involved in international tourism of one kind or another. Countless others were involved in national tourism—going from one part of their country to another.

It's instructive to see where tourists go. In Table 1.1, I list some of the most popular tourist destinations in Europe and Asia for the year 2002. It is difficult to get reliable and up-to-date statistics on tourism. The size of the tourism industry in Asia, even including China, is relatively small, compared, for example, to France and Spain and a number of other European countries. The countries are listed in order of the importance for the tourism industry, with France being in first place and Greece being in fifteenth place (World Tourism Organization, 2002b).

TABLE 1.1. Tourist visits in major destinations (2002).

Country	Tourists (in millions)	Population (in millions)
1. France	77	60.144
2. Spain	51.7	41
3. United States	41.9	294
4. Italy	39.8	57.4
5. China	36.8	1.3 billion
6. United Kingdom	23.9	49.8
7. Canada	20	31.5
8. Mexico	19.7	103
9. Austria	18.6	8.116
10. Germany	18	82.4
11. Hong Kong	16.6	7
Figures below are for 2000		
12. Hungary	15.9	10
13. Greece	13.1	11
14. Poland	17.4	39
15. Malaysia	10.2	23
16. Thailand	10.8	62
17. Vietnam	2.6	81.7
18. Cambodia	66,000 (in thousands)	14

Source: http://www.world-tourism.org.

Table 1.1 suggests that tourism in Thailand, even though it is much larger than Vietnamese and Cambodian tourism, is still relatively underdeveloped, as compared to Western European countries such as France, Spain, and Italy, and other third-world countries, such as Mexico. On a visiting tourist–per capita basis, Austria leads all the countries. With a population of 8 million people, it has approximately the same number of tourists—18 million visitors—as Germany, a country with 82 million people. None of the countries in Southeast Asia are among the fifteen most popular tourist destinations, according to the World Tourism Organization, though with some 10 million tourists, Thailand is not very far behind Greece's 13.1 million international tourists.

Of course, 10 million tourists in a third-world country such as Thailand have, quite likely, a much larger influence on Thai culture and society than 50 million tourists in a first-world country such as France—where tourism has been integrated for many decades into the social system of the country.

TOURIST ARRIVALS TO THAILAND BY NATIONALITY

In Table 1.2, I list the nationalities of visitors to Thailand by country of origin. This allows us to get a better sense of where tourists to Thailand come from. I have selected the major nationalities.

Table 1.2 shows that a relatively small number of countries provide most of the tourists in Thailand. The tourists from Malaysia, while technically international tourists, actually are neighbors of Thailand and their visits may be of short duration and little more than border crossing. The figures do not break down in terms of business travel; so, for instance, the large number of tourists from China may be due to business travel as well as China's proximity to Thailand. These countries provide the bulk of the tourists to Thailand. It also is the case that the United Kingdom, the United States, Germany, France,

TABLE 1.2. Nationalities visiting Thailand.

Country	Number	Percentage
Malaysia	1.3 million	12.25
Japan	1.2 million	11.40
China	790,000	7.34
Korea	704,000	6.48
United Kingdom	704,000	6.48
Taiwan	674,000	6.20
Singapore	576,000	5.03
United States	555,000	5.11
Germany	411,000	3.78
Australia	351,000	3.23
Hong Kong	335,000	3.09
India	280,000	2.58
France	274,000	2.50

Source: Author's compilation. Adapted from data provided by Immigration Bureau, Police Department, Thailand.

and Japan are the countries in which the most money is spent, on a per capita basis, on tourism. The other countries tend to be among the more affluent countries and thus people there have the income to spend money on international tourism.

WORLD'S TOP INTERNATIONAL TOURISM EARNERS

It turns out that Thailand, while it is eighteenth on the list of most popular international tourist destinations, ranks fifteenth when it comes to earnings from international tourism. The top twenty countries, in terms of earnings from international tourism in 2002, are found in Table 1.3, with expenses in U.S. dollars.

TABLE 1.3. World's top international tourism earners.

Country	Receipts (in billions)	Market share (percent)	Population (in millions)	Per capita receipts (in millions)
1. United States	66.5	14.0	288	231
2. Spain	33.6	7.1	40	837
3. France	32.3	6.8	60	539
4. Italy	26.9	5.7	58	465
5. China	20.4	4.3	1,279	16
6. United Kingdom	17.6	3.7	60	294
7. Austria	11.2	2.4	8	1,375
8. Hong Kong	10.1	2.1	7	1,385
9. Greece	9.7	2.1	11	915
10. Canada	9.7	2.0	32	304
11. Turkey	9.0	1.9	67	134
12. Mexico	8.9	1.9	103	86
13. Australia	8.1	1.7	20	414
14. Thailand	7.9	1.7	64	124
15. Netherlands	7.7	1.6	16	480
16. Switzerland	7.6	1.6	7	1,045
17. Belgium	6.9	1.5	10	671
18. Malaysia	6.8	1.4	23	299
19. Portugal	5.9	1.2	10	587
20. Denmark	5.8	1.2	5	1,078

Source: http://www.world-tourism.org.

Thailand, then, is the major tourist attraction in Southeast Asia, earning approximately 8 billion dollars a year on tourism. The top six countries earn about 40 percent on all international tourism expenditures—almost as much as the rest of the countries combined.

What Thailand and other Asian countries have going for them is the fact that many tourists from relatively affluent Western countries are getting tired of visiting Europe and the United States and are looking for something new, which explains why tourism in Thailand has been growing rapidly, despite the problems it faces—terrorism, restive Muslim populations in the south, and Asian bird flu (which impacts tourism in all Asian countries, to varying degrees).

WORLD'S TOP FIFTEEN INTERNATIONAL TOURISM SPENDERS

The World Tourism Organization provides a list of the countries that spend the most on tourism (Table 1.4). The countries are listed in order of amount spent on international tourism. These figures are for 2001 and list the countries in terms of rank of expenditures.

TABLE 1.4. International tourism expenditures.

Country	2001 (billions of U.S. dollars)
United States	58.9
Germany	46.2
United Kingdom	38.5
Japan	26.5
France	17.7
Italy	14.2
China	13.1
Hong Kong	12.5
Netherlands	12.0
Canada	11.6
Belgium	9.8
Austria	8.9
Republic of Korea	6.9
Sweden	6.8
Switzerland	6.6

Source: http://www.world-tourism.org.

The United States might spend the most on international tourism, but it has a population of around 290 million people, in contrast to Germany, with 82 million people. So relatively speaking, Germany and a number of other countries listed in Table 1.4 spend a great deal more (on a per capita basis), than the United States does, on international travel.

VACATION DAYS PER YEAR IN SELECTED COUNTRIES

We must keep in mind that Americans have many fewer vacation days than citizens of Italy, France, and a number of other countries. A list of the average number of vacation days for some of the more important traveling nations can be found in Table 1.5.

So Americans trail the world by a huge margin in terms of the number of days of vacation they have during the year. If we assume a five-day week, Italians get almost eight weeks of vacation a year, the French and the Germans get approximately seven weeks a year, and Americans get a bit more than two weeks a year.

WHAT TOURISTS SPEND IN THAILAND

The Tourism Authority of Thailand (TAT) has prepared a chart on tourism in Thailand from 1996 to 2005. In Table 1.6, I offer some data from that chart for 2002 (in millions where relevant) for international visitors.

What is interesting, if you look at the figures in Table 1.6 for the amount of time international visitors spend in Thailand, is that you

TABLE 1.5. Paid vacation days per year.

Days	Country
14	USA
24	UK
27	Germany
39	France

Source: Author's compilation taken from "Strange Planet: The Curious World of Travel" in *National Geographic Traveler,* p. 124, September 2006.

TABLE 1.6. Data on visitors to Thailand.

Number	Change	Length of stay	Expenditure in baht	Change	Revenue	Change
10,8	+5.82	7.98 days	3,754	+0.16	323,484	+8.17

Source: Adapted from data provided by the Tourism Authority of Thailand (TAT).

find that the average visitor to Thailand stays approximately eight days and spends approximately 3,800 baht per day. At approximately 40 baht per dollar, that amounts to less than a 100 dollars a day, a figure that is probably low due to the number of backpackers in Thailand. (In November of 2004, 3,800 baht equaled 94 U.S. dollars.) If the average tourist in Thailand stays there 8 days and spends around 100 dollars a day, the average visitor there spends $800 during his or her visit. If you multiply this by 10 million, the estimated number of visitors in Thailand in 2004, you get around 8 billion dollars that tourism contributes to Thailand's economy. Tourism is the largest industry in Thailand, and the Thai government is doing everything it can to attract more tourists to Thailand.

The people of modern Thailand are as varied as the populations of many nations of the world. They come in all shapes and sizes, complexions and statures, and include farmers and computer programmers, soldiers and bus drivers, merchants and students, princes and monks. Virtually all would, when asked, call themselves "Thai" and, in using this term, would imply a definition primarily political: they are "Thai" as citizens of Thailand, subjects of the Thai king. If pressed, they might extend their definition further, to give the term a cultural and linguistic sense, and be "Thai" as a speaker of the Thai language and a participant in Thai culture. All the things that make up "Thai" identity, however, have developed only slowly through many centuries, and none of the things to which the modern Thai now refers—political, cultural, linguistic—existed in its present form until relatively recently.

Wyatt, *Thailand: A Short History,* 1984

The marketing of Thai culture domestically and to foreign visitors subsidizes or underwrites the cost of efforts to preserve Thai culture, seen to be under threat by Western ways. Like many developing countries with rich heritages, Thailand sells itself abroad by commodifying its culture and tradition. . . . Heritage and tradition are simultaneously trivialized, celebrated and exploited. Similarly, Thai women in their essentialized Bangkok guise have been used both to represent tradition, at times an invented tradition, and as signs of civilization with their high heels and hats. This basic paradox permeates Thai gender representations.

Van Esterik, *Materializing Thailand,* 2002: 124

Chapter 2

Typical Tourist Itineraries
in Thailand

Once people have decided to visit Thailand, they have to determine where to go in a country about the size of France. In many countries, there are certain cities and places that almost all tourists visit, and the same applies to Thailand. Some tourists love beaches and head to various Thai beaches and spend all their time there. Others are interested in Thai culture and take what are sometimes described as "Classical Thai Tours." What interests me is where the average tourist interested in exploring Thai culture goes.

To answer this question, I examined a number of tours of Thailand that are offered by various tourism companies, both American and Thai. In this chapter I list and compare what might be described as the "classic" tours of Thailand.

THE CLASSIC TOURS OF THAILAND

In Table 2.1, I list the places that four tours of Thailand visit. The first three tour companies are American and the last one is Thai (although the company is actually Vietnamese). The prices do not always include airport taxes and other similar expenses. So one has to add about 150 dollars for the SmarTours and Gate 1 tours of Thailand.

What Table 2.1 indicates is that there are considerable similarities in the places that these tourist companies take tourists in Thailand, but there are also a number of differences. What is interesting is that the AsianAdventure tour, at 810 dollars, turns out to be more expen-

Thailand Tourism
© 2007 by The Haworth Press, Inc. All rights reserved.
doi:10.1300/5789_02

TABLE 2.1. Classic tours of Thailand.

Overseas Adv. Travel	SmarTours	Gate1	AsianAdventure
16 days	14 days	12 days	10 days
$1595-$1995	$899-$999	$999-$1129	$810 (plus airfare)
Bangkok	Bangkok	Bangkok	Bangkok
Kanchanaburi	Ayuthaya	Ayuthaya	Ayuthaya
Uthathani	Phitsanulok	Saraburi	Chiang Mai
Phitsanuloke	Sukothai	Lopburi	Pae
Sukothai	Lampang	Phitsanulok	Mae Hong Son
Phrae	Phayao	Lampang	Chiang Rai
Chiang Rai	Mae Sai	Phayan	Bangkok
Mae Salong	Chiang Rai	Chiang Rai	
Chiang Mai	Chiang Mai	Chiang Mai	
Bangkok	Bangkok	Bangkok	

Source: Author's compilation.

sive than the other tours, which include airfare from San Francisco or other cities in the United States (at an additional charge). The charges for these tours rise during the high season in Thailand—though not all tourism companies agree when the high season is.

I have not included all the places where the tours stop on the way from one city to another. Thus, for example, the AsianAdventure tour stops in Chiang Saen and Mae Sai on its way to Chiang Rai and its return to Bangkok. So there are variations of one sort or another, but all tours start in Bangkok and end there as well, and all go to Chiang Mai and Chiang Rai.

COMMONALITIES OF THE FOUR TOURS

We can get an idea of the similarities and differences among the four tours by looking at the Table 2.2, which shows commonalities in the tours.

What this reveals is that different tours stop at different places along the way as they head to Chiang Rai and Chiang Mai and the "Golden Triangle," but the general contours of each itinerary are similar. The shorter tours do not have as much time to spend on side trips to this or that place of interest.

TABLE 2.2. Commonalties in tours of Thailand.

Four tours	Three tours	Two tours
Bangkok	Ayuthaya	Sukothai
Chiang Mai	Phitsanulok	Lampang
Chiang Rai		

Source: Author's compilation, based on travel literature of tours in Thailand by various tourism companies.

A SUGGESTED TOUR OF THAILAND BY A THAI TOURISM STUDENT

This itinerary was sent to me by an informant of mine, a Thai woman who is a PhD candidate in tourism studies in Australia. Her dissertation advisor, with whom I have corresponded over the years, told her that I was interested in what were the most important sites in Thailand, and she suggested the following places.

Thailand Itinerary As Proposed by Thai Tourism Scholar

1. Central Thailand

Bangkok
   a. The Grand Royal Palace.
   b. The Temple of the Emerald Buddha (Wat Phra-kaew)—exquisite Emerald Buddha, colorful mosaics and glittering spires.
   c. The Temple of Dawn (Wat Arun)—viewing Bangkok and Chao Phraya River from top of the stupa.
   d. Wat Pho—houses Thailand's largest reclining Buddha and school for Thai traditional massage/yoga.
   e. National museum.
   f. Vimarnmek Teak Mansion—L-shaped three-storey mansion that served as King Rama V's residence. It contains eighty-one rooms, halls, and anterooms and is said to be the world's largest teak building. The mansion contains various personal effects of the king and a treasure trove of Rattanakosin art objects and antiques. (Note: a, b, c, d, and e are in the same area.)

Ayutthaya Province
  a. Ayutthaya World Heritage Site/Park (the ancient capital).
  b. Chao Sam Phraya National Museum.
  c. Wat Panancheng—sacred temple southeast of town on Chao Phraya river. The main *wihaan* contains a highly revered sitting Buddha image.
  d. Wat Yai Chai Mongkhon—it contains a very large *chedis* and a large reclining Buddha image.

Bang-Pa
  a. Bang Pa-In Palace, Bang Pa-In district—20 km south of the town, it has a collection of palace buildings in a wide variety of architectural styles.
  b. Wat Niwet ThampraWat, Bang Pa-In district across the river from the south of Bang Pa-In Palace grounds, is Wat Niwet ThampraWat. This temple represents a Gothic Christian church architecture.

Phetburi Province (Bangkok's nearest seaside province)
  a. Chaam Beach.
  b. Hua-Hin Beach.
  c. Khow Wang Palace.

Chonburi Province (east of Bangkok)
  a. Pattaya beach for 3Ss: sea/sun/sand and night life.

2. Northern Thailand

Chiang Mai
  a. Wat Phra That Doi Suthep on Doi Suthep. Visit sacred temple where the holy relics of Lord Buddha have been kept.
  b. Wat Phra Sing: The *wihaan* of this temple is a perfect example of the classic Northern Thai (Lanna period).
  c. Wat Suan Dok: It contains a 500-year-old bronze Buddha image and murals depicting Buddha's life story.
  d. Wat Chedi Luang or the monastery of the Great stupa.
  e. Chiang Mai National Museum.

Wat Phra That Doi Suthep near Chiang Mai

Chiang Rai
Most of the tourist attractions in Chiang Rai are out of town.
   a. Golden Triangle.
   b. The Grand Mom's Royal Palace on Mae Fa Luang.
   c. Doi Mae Salong: Visit hill tribes and taste some tea.
   d. Border market at Mae Sai district.

Tour attractions out of town
   a. Handicrafts villages in Sankamphaeng district and Ban
      Thawai village in Sarapee district.
   b. Chiang Dao Elephant Jungle Trek at Chiang Dao Ele-
      phant Camp.
   c. Mae Sa Valley: Visit orchid farms/butterfly farms/rain-
      forest reptiles farm and many beautiful resorts on the way.
   d. Doi Inthanon: The highest mountain in Thailand, well
      known for bird watching.

Another view of Wat Phra That Doi Suthep

3. Northeastern Thailand

   a. Ban Chiang World Heritage in Udonthani.
   b. Nong Khai—viewing Mae Khong River and visiting markets.

4. Southern Thailand (diving, sea-canoeing, water activities, etc.)

   a. Phuket island, Phuket Province.
   b. Samui island, Surathani Province.
   c. Krabi province.

Most of the activities in these three southern provinces are diving, sea-canoeing, and water activities.

* * *

Tourist companies with their "classical" or northern Thai tours visit many of the places mentioned on this list. Tourists who are planning to visit Thailand on their own can benefit from the advice of an expert and plan their visits using the list. There are also lists in guidebooks such as the *Lonely Planet Thailand* or *Rough Guides Thailand* for tours of varying lengths of time.

INTREPID TOURS IN THAILAND

American tourist companies generally offer one tour of Thailand, the "classic" tour, which I discussed earlier. But some tourist companies, such as Intrepid Travel, offer more than a dozen different tours of Thailand—from short, five-day stays in beach resorts to twenty-three-day tours of both northern and southern Thailand, often involving three-day treks in the hill country, along with such traditional tourist experiences as trips on rice barges and elephant riding. In Table 2.3, I list the descriptions used by this company for many of its tours (duration is in terms of days).

TABLE 2.3. Selected Intrepid tours of Thailand.

Duration	Description
12	Premium Thailand
15	Northern Thailand
8	Tap Into Thailand
8	A Taste of Thailand
15	Tribal Thailand
8	A Taste of Adventure
8	Treasures of the North
15	Villages and Islands
5	Coral Bay Resort
5	Krabi Beach Break
10	Thailand Gourmet Traveller
18	Thailand Unplugged
23	Thailand Encompassed
21	Temples and Beaches
15	Thai Family Adventure
28	Thailand North and South
24	Siam Sunset

Source: Intrepid tours. Adapted from www.Intrepidtravel.com.

Author's compilation, taken from a brochure of tours of Thailand offered by Intrepid Tours.

From this list you can see that there are an enormous number of ways to tour in Thailand with this company, from short stays on islands with beautiful beaches to tours focusing on Thai cuisine to extended tours of Thailand's classic sites, which may involve three-day treks and overnight stays with Thai families.

The Intrepid Adventure tours are not high-end tours, for the most part, and Intrepid rates each of them in terms of culture shock and how strenuous they are. They seem designed primarily for young people and backpackers. Many Thai tour companies offer a variety of different tours as well—similar in nature to the Intrepid tours.

It seems, then, that the tourism industry in Thailand is highly developed relative to most other Southeast Asian countries, and Thailand is the dominant country in Southeast Asia as far as international tourism is concerned. On the Web page (2004) of the Intrepid Travel site for Thailand (www.intrepidtravel.com/destination.php?region= thailand) there is a postage-stamp-sized photo of Dtor Dtae, one of Intrepid's guides in Thailand. She writes:

> I am Thai. As a child, my mother and I would walk into the paddy fields at night search for tasty frogs, fish and grasshoppers under the moonlight. There were no paved roads, electricity or electrical devices, but we were never bored. Our days were filled with the sweet scent of steamed rice, the crunch of fresh forest vegetables and the sounds of laughter.

If you press the "Read More" note, she continues about how different life is in Bangkok, where she studied. Her description of her early years in a paradise-like Thailand is one of the dominant themes, I would suggest, resonating in the minds of tourists when they decide to visit Thailand. As the Overseas Adventure Travel brochure puts it:

> In Thailand—once called Siam—independence, hospitality, and the traditional philosophy that "life is pleasure" weave a spell on every visitor.

It is this "life is pleasure" spell that Thailand weaves which I will be investigating, among other things, in this book. I say that because all trips we take involve an imagined trip or fantasized trip and then the actual trip, and the difference between the two can be considerable—since our experiences in life seldom live up to the fantasies we have about them.

THE SNAKE OF TERRORISM IN THE PARADISE OF THAILAND, AND OTHER PROBLEMS

After the attack by terrorists on another Asian paradise, Bali, many people canceled their trips to Thailand, and in some areas tourism dried up to remarkable proportions. In an article by Seth Mydans and Keith Bradsher in the November 12, 2002, *The New York Times,* they write about more than 30,000 room nights being canceled at a cost of around 3 million dollars for Thai hotel keepers. Europeans, Americans, and Australians, they write, stayed away from Thailand and many other Southeast Asian countries such as Malaysia, Singapore, Laos, and Cambodia.

The Thai authorities responded by budgeting a million dollars for advertising—reassuring tourists that Thailand was safe and forming a special antiterrorist command, which, the authors suggest, never really got off the ground. Thailand's tourism industry grew at 6 percent after the September 11, 2001, attacks in the United States and reached 10.3 million visitors in 2001. So it managed to attract tourists, even though, for a while, there was panic—affecting both the people running the tourist sites in Thailand and in the minds of potential tourists to Thailand.

As I write this book, in 2005, there is trouble in southern Thailand, where most of the Muslim Thais live and this, along with the Asian bird flu and the tsunami disaster, has impacted the tourist trade to some degree. What has happened is that many tourists avoid areas where there are perceived dangers from restive Muslim populations and keep away from any country where there is news about the bird flu. The danger of the Asian bird flu is that if it spreads to human beings it might very well lead to a worldwide pandemic in which it has been estimated that between 20 million and a 100 million people will die. There is also the matter of the tsunami disaster of December 26, 2004, which has impacted tourism in Thailand, though the long-term effects of this disaster are hard to assess.

On the other hand, the threat of terrorism is now so ubiquitous that many tourists do not think about it very much, or do not consider it to be all important. Terrorism is one more problem tourists have to factor into their thinking when they plan their trips. Terrorists have killed people in Spain, in Bali, in Egypt, in New York, and many other popular tourist sites. Therefore, many people now conclude that no place is safe, which, ironically, means every place (with certain obvious exceptions, such as Israel and Iraq and various African countries) is approximately as safe and as dangerous as any other place. So almost every place is now open to being visited.

Thailand, it has been suggested, preferred to avert its eyes to the terrorism threat and did not respond to it seriously. Every visitor to Thailand knows that the terrorists might strike Thailand but, like the Thais, these tourists avert their eyes (after having factored in the dangers involved) as well, factor in the risks, hope for the best, and concentrate on being happy in "The Land of Smiles."

Siam, about the size of France, is a country of rice, rubber, fourteen million good-natured peasants, and a boy king. On the map it looks rather like an octopus with one tentacle dangling into Malay toward Singapore. It is the country where no one needs to work more than three or four months a year (because the climate is so propitious and rice so abundant), where the pronunciation of names is fantastically at variance with spelling (for instance "Guamchitphol" is pronounced "Kunchit"), where Japanese influence is increasingly active, where there are 17,408 monasteries and 225,000 priests, and where white elephants are sacred.

Its capital, the town of Bangkok, is a charming place where tramcars are yellow and the priests' robes orange, where one-fifth of the total area is covered by temples, where rice husks are used as fuel, where silver plated tiger skulls are sold as ash trays, where rickshas are drawn by bicycles, and where you put your feet in bags up to the thighs to keep the mosquitoes off.

Siam is the only independent country in Asia between Japan and Persia, the only eastern territory that did not become booty of the great powers during the imperialistic expansion of the nineteenth century. The Siamese call their country "Muang-Thai," which means land of the free.

John Gunther, Inside Asia, 1939: 332

For some reason, heat and sensuality go hand in hand . . . and the heat in Bangkok, where the Thai start donning sweaters when the temperature drops below 85 degrees, is an extraordinary kind. Five minutes in it and you are drenched to the skin. After an hour your mind is on its way to being parboiled. It starts playing tricks. The noisy *tuk-tuks,* which from the tinted-glass windows of the air-conditioned hire-car seemed like to many three-wheeled menaces, take on an inexplicable charm.

Robert Sam Anson, "Sixth Sense" in James O'Reilly
and Larry Habegger, eds., Traveler's Tales Thailand, 2002: 6

Chapter 3

Images of Thailand
in Travel Literature

In this chapter I discuss the way Thailand has been portrayed in travel literature—providing what might be described as an "image" of Thailand that tourists pick up as they read through books on Thailand by scholars and travel writers and as they see images of Thailand in films, television shows, and travel advertising.

JOHN GUNTHER'S SIAM

It is rather curious to read John Gunther's description of Siam/Thailand in his book *Inside Asia*. It was published more than sixty years ago and describes a Thailand that seems more like a storybook kingdom than a real country. Gunther's Thailand was a small country of peasants who only needed to work three or four months a year, due to the bountiful nature of the land and the propitious climate.

He is taken up by the fact that Thailand was never a colonial country—a very important matter for Thais and one that many commentators have suggested helps explain Thai national character. He described a bloodless revolution that took place in which the only casualty was a general who was wounded in the leg. This was because the Siamese are, as Gunther puts it, a "mild people."

This picture that Gunther presents is one of Thailand as a kind of Polynesian paradise, where the people are simple folk living, one might imagine, in a state of natural grace, in thatched roofs huts and not needing to work very hard—only three or four months a year—

Thailand Tourism
doi:10.1300/5789_03

An old rice mill

to survive. The image seems quite bizarre to us when we think of modern Thailand, with a population of 61 million people and a huge megalopolis, Bangkok, full of skyscrapers, traffic jams, and terrible pollution.

The images of a country we get from travelers are always somewhat suspect, and Gunther's Siam is probably a rather fantastic picture of the country. Still, he did notice the importance of the fact that Thailand was the only country in Southeast Asia never to have been a colony and was fascinated by the number of monks and the amount of land Thai temples occupied. Whether his figures were accurate is difficult to say.

THE LONELY PLANET GUIDEBOOKS

Earlier I quoted the first paragraph in the book, from the Introduction in the fourth edition of the Lonely Planet guide to Thailand. The first paragraph in the 2003 edition reads as follows:

The Kingdom of Thailand draws more visitors than any other country in Southeast Asia with its virtually irresistible combination of breathtaking natural beauty, inspiring temples, the ruins of fabulous ancient Kingdoms, renowned hospitality, and robust cuisine. (2003: 11)

A few paragraphs later, it discusses the Thais as fun-loving and cites, in an updated and slightly modified version, a number of descriptions of Thais and Thailand borrowed from the earlier version of the book.

If you look at the language in the 2003 edition, you notice that the adjectives are all very strong and extremely positive: irresistible, breathtaking, inspiring, fabulous, renowned, and robust. These superlatives offer an image of a country that almost demands to be visited and, as such, make purchasing the guidebook, for anyone who might be looking at the book in a bookstore, for example, a necessity. Thus, as it sells Thailand, it sells itself.

Describing countries in terms of superlatives is, it would seem, one of the conventions of Lonely Planet guidebooks and probably most guidebooks. Writers of these guidebooks have to sell the country in order to sell their guidebooks to that country. To show this, let me quote from the Introduction to the *Lonely Planet Vietnam, Fifth Edition:*

Vietnam, a country made famous by war, has a unique and rich civilization, spectacular scenery and a highly cultured, cordial people. . . . Most visitors to Vietnam are overwhelmed by the sublime beauty of the country's natural setting. The Red River Delta in the north, the Mekong Delta in the south and almost the entire coastal strip are a patchwork of brilliant green rice paddies tended by peasant women in conical hats. Vietnam's 3451 km coastline includes countless kilometers of unspoiled beaches and a number of stunning lagoons. . . . Visitors to Vietnam have their senses thrilled by all the sights, sounds, tastes and smells of a society which has both survived and been re-created by a century of contact (to put it mildly) between ancient civilization and the modern ways of the west. (1999: 11)

Scene from a ruin in Thailand

My point, then, is that the writers of guidebooks for Lonely Planet, and for other companies selling guidebooks and tourist agencies, tend to deal in superlatives—raising very high expectations in the minds of people who read these books and some of those who visit the countries described in the guidebooks. Later on in these guidebooks there are pages about the various dangers involved in traveling in these countries, which travelers tend to discount.

In the case of Vietnam and Thailand, and other countries as well, I would surmise that many of the expectations readers get of these countries from guidebooks and brochures are tempered by a realization most people have that their travels in these countries will not be—and cannot be—as "fabulous" as the guidebooks and advertisements suggest they will be. This is tied to a tendency we learn, as we grow up, to discount—to some degree—the claims made by advertisers and others about products and services being advertised.

Still, most tourists go to Thailand hoping to have a good time and the guidebooks are correct in asserting that Thailand does, in fact, have a great deal to offer—more than just sun, sand, sea, sex, and shopping though, for some tourists, that is essentially what they are interested in.

THREE THAI CONCEPTS

In *The Rough Guide to Thailand,* Paul Gray and Lucy Ridout offer some insights into the Thai personality and Thai attitudes, which are meant to help tourists in Thailand adjust to some of the facts of life in that country. They write:

> There are three specifically Thai concepts you're bound to come across and which may help you to comprehend a sometimes laissez-faire attitude to delayed buses and other inconveniences. The first, *jai yen,* translates literally as "cool heart" and is something everyone tries to maintain—most Thais hate raised voices, visible irritation and confrontations of any kind. Related to this is the oft-quoted response to a difficulty, *mai pen rai*—"never mind," "no problem," or "it can't be helped—the verbal equivalent of an open-handed shoulder shrug which has its base in the Buddhist notion of karma. And then there's *sanuk,* the wide-reaching philosophy of "fun" which, crass as it sounds, Thai do their best to inject into any situation, even work. Hence the crowds of inebriated Thais who congregate at Waterfalls and other beauty spots on public holidays, and the national Water-fight which takes place every April on streets right across Thailand. (*Rough Guide to Thailand,* quoted in James O'Reilly and Larry Habegger, eds., 2002: 4)

These three concepts help explain a great deal about Thai culture and personality. Thai society is permeated by Buddhism, which preaches abstinence and piety, yet we find a culture in which there is a kind of carefree lassitude that informs it (at least on the surface)—much to the consternation of many tourists, who are used to having buses run on time and who believe that when problems arise, they should be fixed, not shrugged off. Buddhism, Thais suggest, does not forbid pleasure—just inflicting pain. Buddhism's influence and beliefs are discussed in more detail in Chapter 6.

These sights and experiences that contrast with what we expect, with our sense of "normalcy," are what culture shock is all about. We are shocked when we find ourselves confronting belief structures and modes of behavior that vary with those that we bring with us, and part of the joy of travel involves finding these "shocks" and, if they are not too great, not too overwhelming, learning how to deal with them.

PICO IYER ON THAILAND'S COMPLEXITIES

Pico Iyer, one of the most astute and sophisticated of contemporary travel writers, deals with Thailand in his book *Video Night in Katmandu.* He has a chapter that focuses on bar girls and prostitutes, and recognizes that the relationships between prostitutes and the men who use their services are much more complex than we might imagine. As he explains:

> Before very long, in fact, I began to discover that the ubiquitous couple of Bangkok—the pudgy foreigner, with the exquisite girleen—was not quite the buyer and seller, the subject and object, I had imagined. In many cases, I was told, the girls did not simply make their bodies available to all while they looked at their watches and counted their money; they chose to offer their admirers their time, their thoughts, even their lives. The couple would sometimes stay together for two weeks, or three, or thirty. (Iyer, 2004: 20)

Thus, Iyer's "paradigm," which involved the West exploiting the East, started falling apart. Tourists, like anyone, make sense of the new in terms of the old; they make sense of what they find in Thailand by comparing it with what they know about their own country and other countries they visit. In a sense, then, we can say that tourists know what a country is not, but that does not necessarily help them know what a country is.

Iyer writes about a number of prostitutes he met and is rather sympathetic toward them, generally speaking. Not all were the kind who, as he put it, could be "touched anyplace except inside." If there is a theme that informs Iyer's essay it is that he discovered that he was mistaken about the seemingly clear-cut oppositions that he thought were operating in Thailand. As he writes about Bangkok:

> . . . At last, I thought, there was one clear-cut division here, in the Manichean setup of Bangkok. The city's two most common and appealing sights, after all, were its holy men in spotless saffron robes, and its scarlet ladies. By day, the monks evoked a vision of purity, of hallowed groves filled with golden novitiates; by night, the whole grimy city felt polished, renewed, and transformed as sequined girls sang the body electric. At least, so I thought, this day-and-night division would ensure that good was good, and evil evil, and never the twain would meet.

> But no. For after a while, I began to notice that, as the whores were engagingly girlish, the monks seemed endearingly boyish. I saw them pouring over Walkmans in electronic stores with shopping bags slung over their shoulders, puffing ruminatively on cigarettes, playing tag with their friends in temple courtyards. . . . Thus the real sorcery of this dizzying place was that before one knew it, it could work on one not just a physical but a moral seduction. For here was a decadence so decorous that it disarmed the criticism it invited: amorality expressed with the delicacy of a ballerina's nod. (Iyer, 2002: 29-30)

In trying to understand Bangkok and Thailand, Iyer saw himself as not so much in the dark, but in the shadows—not being able to fully comprehend the mysterious contradictions of Thai culture. These enigmatic contradictions are part of Thailand's mysterious allure, part of what fascinates tourists so much about the country.

In his book *Thai Tourism: Hill Tribes, Islands and Open-Ended Prostitution,* Erik Cohen describes some of the complicated relationships that exist between Thai prostitutes and their clients as "open-ended," suggesting that in some cases, and chance plays an important role here, the women develop short-term and, sometimes, relatively long-term relationships with the men they sleep with. So the sex trade in Thailand is much more complicated than one might imagine, and is not a matter of one-directional exploitation. Pico Iyer's attempt to understand how prostitutes lived in Thailand and to make sense of their relationships with the men who used their services recognizes some of the complexities involved in these relationships.

SLOGANS

After two years of using "Amazing Thailand" as its slogan, the Tourism Authority of Thailand has replaced it with a new slogan, "Happiness on Earth." This information comes from an article in the *Bangkok Post* on the Internet that quoted Jutamas Siriwan, the governor of the Tourism Authority of Thailand, as saying:

> When people think of traveling, they expect happiness. And Thailand just matches this criteria. That is how the slogan was coined. This time we have been more careful in choosing the words for this campaign. Unlike Amazing Thailand which can carry both positive and negative connotation, we're sure that "happiness" can only have a positive effect.

She announced this slogan at the World Travel Market in London, held during November 8-11, 2004. This notion that Thailand is "Happiness on Earth" fits in with my suggestion that there is a somewhat diluted Garden of Eden paradisical aspect to popular notions people have about Thailand.

What the slogan does not do is use the name of the country; so the slogan is somewhat indirect in selling Thailand as a place to visit. But it will be used in advertisements and commercials about Thailand; so the fact that Thailand is not mentioned in the slogan probably is not terribly important. The "Happiness" theme also calls to mind "Happy Hours" in bars, which connote sociability, relaxation, and pleasure. The slogan "Amazing Thailand" implied superlatives, though Siriwan's notion that it also could have negative connotations is reasonable. Ko Samui's beaches may be amazing, but so are Bangkok's traffic jams.

In essence, the "Happiness on Earth" slogan takes us back to John Gunther's picture of Siam as an Asian paradise full of happy people. The new slogan suggests to tourists that when they visit Thailand, they, too, will be able to partake of the "happiness" that is such an important element of life in Siam/Thailand. The Thai people are often described, in travel literature, as a "happy-go-lucky" people. But how happy are the Thai people? In Chapter 4, I deal with some interesting aspects of Thai national character, culture, and personality.

Thailand is changing fast. It used to be thought of as a gorgeous El Dorado of gilded Buddhas and the chromatic sheen of Thai silk, a paradise of sweet frangipani and tall languid palm trees rippling in the sunshine, a land of graceful people and soft smiles. For many tourists that is still how Thailand appears. This mysterious and charming kingdom has progressed so far, however, in modernizing itself and building an industrial base that is personality has altered. The old glamour is still there, but is increasingly obscured by the overlay of modern economic and international life. . . . Millions of Americans and Europeans have gone on holiday in Thailand to be charmed by its physically attractive people and their beguiling ambiguity. The Thais missed out on the puritan experience which so inhibited the West. Their attitude toward the natural world, including sex, is spontaneous and guiltless. . . . Thai society has a distinctive composition. It is hierarchical, with the king at its pinnacle, yet it allows a good measure of personal independence with that hierarchy. The Thais are more individualistic than either the Chinese of the Japanese. On the other hand they do not treat each other as equals. Western individualism means little to them.

Kulick and Wilson, *Thailand's Turn:*
Profile of a New Dragon, 1992: 1

The Thais, wrote Le Carré, are the world's swiftest and most efficient killers. Yet executioners would shoot their victims through gauze so as not to offend the Buddha, and monks would strain their water through their teeth so as not, by chance, to harm a single insect.

Pico Iyer, *Video Night in Katmandu,*1998

Chapter 4

Violence and Marriage in Thailand: Two Aspects of Thai Character, Culture, and Personality

The aforementioned quotation, from Kulick and Wilson's *Thailand's Turn,* captures many interesting aspects of Thai character and culture and helps explain why Thailand is such an enigmatic and fascinating society for Western tourists, and probably tourists from other Asian countries as well. Thailand was seen by many tourists, and is still seen by others, they point out, as a kind of tropical paradise. But that image is only part of the story, because, as a new "dragon," Thailand has been industrializing and modernizing, and the factory and sky-scraper are now also an important part of the landscape, along with the *wats,* the tall palm trees, and the tropical beaches we see in travel brochures about Thailand.

THE "HAPPY-GO-LUCKY" THAIS AND THE BURMESE

I quote a passage from the Introduction to the *Lonely Planet Thailand,* in which the authors discuss Thai personality:

> Often depicted as fun-loving, happy-go-lucky folk (which indeed they often are), the Thais are also proud and strong, and have struggled for centuries to preserve their independence of spirit. (11)

Thailand Tourism
© 2007 by The Haworth Press, Inc. All rights reserved.
doi:10.1300/5789_04

When I read this passage I recalled an interesting discussion of Burma found in Victor Barnouw's classic text *Culture and Personality*. In this book, in a section devoted to Economic and Political Development in Burma, he mentions the work of two scholars, Everett E. Hagen and Lucian W. Pye, who have studied Burma and noted:

> Both authors drew attention to the seeming contradiction of mild, carefree, happy-go-lucky behavior among Burmese on the one hand and a high rate of violence and homicide on the other. Hagen is struck by the sluggishness of Burma's economic development, while Pye is concerned with psychological obstacles to "nation building" in Burma. . . . The happy-go-lucky behavior of Burmese is interpreted by Hagen as a defense against repressed rage. Pye considers the manifest level of Burmese politics to be characterized by friendliness and the latent level by tension. Hatred and violence may flare up without warming. Political power is highly valued by the Burmese. At the same time, a power seeker is held back by the need to show deference and respect for others, a conflict which brings about feelings of paralysis and resentment. . . . There is an individualistic stress in this society. According to Pye, the idea of improving the national economy has little meaning for Burmese. People are oriented to the present and have little sense of history or concern with planning for the future. (1973: 466-468)

Although written more than thirty years ago, this discussion of Burmese culture and society made me wonder whether there were strong similarities between the characters of Burmese and of Thais—two neighboring countries with many so-called happy-go-lucky people. Both countries stress on individualism and seem to lack a well-developed civic sensibility, though Thailand is an economic powerhouse and Burma's economy is moribund.

VIOLENCE IN THAI SOCIETY

I wondered, in particular, whether there was any relationship between the Thai smile, the Thai easygoing nature (as shown in public, that is), and violence. A bit of searching on the Internet showed that like the Burmese, as described in 1973, Thai culture is also very violent. A study of homicides per 100,000 people in 2000 offered the following statistics as shown in Table 4.1.

So Thailand ranks third in number of homicides per 100,000 people. Japan, not listed in Table 4.2, was at the bottom of the list with 1.1 murders per 100,000 people.

In a study of homicides with firearms in 2000, we find the statistics as shown in Table 4.2.

In 2000, there were 5,135 murders in Thailand while in the United States, in 2002, there were 16,204 murders. I used the 2000 figure for Thailand because I could not obtain figures for 2002. Since the United States has approximately five times as many people in Thailand, if you multiply the figure for Thailand by five you get approximately 25,000 murders of all kinds.

It seems reasonable to suggest, then, that there may be certain similarities between Burmese and Thai culture, which would suggest that the famous Thai smile might be the social face that Thais present to the world, and that behind it is a considerable amount of repressed anger and hostility. That might help explain the chaotic nature of Thai politics, as well. There are obviously differences, as well. Unlike the Burmese, the Thais have industrialized and become a Southeast

TABLE 4.1. Homicides per 100,000 people.

Country	Homicides per 100,000 people
1. South Africa	117
2. Russian Federation	22
3. Thailand	16.3

Source: Adapted from The Law and Order Referendum (2004) (http://www.laworderreferendum.org.nzl/data.htm).

TABLE 4.2. Homicides with firearms in three countries.

Country	Homicides per 100,000 people
1. South Africa	74.57
2. Thailand	33
3. USA	2.98

Source: Adapted from Sensible Sentencing Trust (2004) (www.Safe-N2.org; accessed November 22, 2004).

Asian "Dragon," and they have a democratic government. But there is reason to suggest that there is a difference between the public face that Thais present to the world and their inner feelings.

The term "personality" has its root in the term *persona* or mask. Our personalities are the masks we use to present ourselves to the world and the Thai mask, I suggest, is the smile. Most of the violence in Thai society is directed at other Thais; so tourists would not generally be exposed to this aspect of Thai society. (I have more to say about the Thai smile in Chapter 6.)

MARRIAGE IN THAILAND AS REFLECTED IN THAI COMIC BOOKS

An article by Andrew Matzner, "Not a Pretty Picture: Images of Married Life in Thai Comic Books," in the *International Journal of Comic Art,* offers some fascinating insights into Thai married life, as reflected in Thai comics. Matzner writes:

> Tattooing, ghosts and spirits, prostitution, development issues, youth trends are all frequent subject matter for cartoonists. I was most struck by how often "the battle between the sexes" appeared as a theme. Gender issues are extremely common subject matter, and those which are centered around marriage are especially prevalent. Significantly, husbands are consistently portrayed as pathetic figures, frequently bullied (both verbally and physically) by no-nonsense wives. . . . Marriage is portrayed in comics as a site of tension and even hostility between the sexes. Husbands are overwhelmingly portrayed as victims and dupes, while wives are characterized as strong, asexual bullies. (2000: 57-58)

Matzner points out that relations between the sexes are portrayed in the Thai comics as quite different while they are dating, but after marriage, the character flaws of each partner are revealed, life takes a decidedly different turn.

In the comics, Thai women, after marriage, become asexual, unattractive (often drawn as short and barrel shaped) mother figures who focus their love and attention on their children, while the Thai husband finds his sexual satisfaction with attractive young, tall, and shapely women, prostitutes or "minor" wives *(mia noi)*. It is not unusual in the comics for wives to beat their errant husbands with sarks, blunt kitchen tools, and in some cases, to cut off the penises of their errant husbands. Matzner quotes an article from the 1980 *Straits Times* of interest, "Repairing the Victims of Thai Wives' Knifes":

> Bangkok. Male infidelity is a risky business in Thailand. A Bangkok hospital yesterday opened a medical unit devoted to the reconnection of sexual members severed by jealous wives or fiancees. Mr. Wassan MeeWattha of Siriraj hospital said the special surgery unit had been created because of Thailand's high incidence, probably the highest in the world, of "sexual punishment." The Thai press regularly carries reports of women who deliberately cut off their lovers' sexual organs either out of jealousy or anger. (2000: 71)

It would seem, then, that many Thai women as well as Thai men have a great deal of repressed anger.

CULTURAL EXPLANATIONS

Matzner suggests that one reason for the way gender relations are portrayed in the comics has to do with the former policy of conscripting ordinary men *(prai)* to work for the state in many parts of Thailand, leaving their wives responsible for keeping the family together. As a result, Thai women became very self-sufficient, a trait they passed on to their daughters. Daughters are also trained to be nurturing, responsible, and practical. The Thai mothers also spoiled their sons and developed very intense relationships with them, as a means of sublimating their sexual energies. Thai husbands, then, become more emotionally bonded to their mothers than their wives.

The Thais believe, Matzner adds, that women can control and repress their sexual desires but men cannot, which helps explain why men become involved in extramarital affairs so often. Thai wives consider it acceptable for their husbands to consort with prostitutes, since they are less threatening to the family finances than a "minor" wife.

It is these factors that help explain why Thai comics portray married life the way they do. On the other hand, it is not unusual in American comics and other forms of popular culture to show husbands as weaklings and dupes, and the Thai comics may be using stereotyping and other exaggerated techniques to create humor. But underneath the humor, these comics reveal, it would seem, very strong currents of anger and antipathy as far as husbands and wives are concerned, and may help explain why prostitution in Thailand is such a large industry.

Sexual tourists benefit from Thailand's highly developed prostitution industry and for many years, large groups of tourists came from a number of countries, near and far, with the primary purpose of utilizing this industry. It is Thai family relations and attitudes about sexuality, then, that is one reason why there are so many prostitutes in Thailand. This means, ironically, dysfunctional Thai families are connected, indirectly, to the sex tourism industry in Thailand.

PART II:
SEMIOTIC SIAM

Semiotics is the science of signs. It's most distinctive theoretical characteristic is the negation of the division of subject from object which is the keystone of traditional Western science. Semiotics locates the *sign,* which it treats as an original unification of subject and object, in place of the old subject-object split at the center of scientific investigation. In Charles Sanders Peirce's original formulation, a *sign represents something to someone.*

I have suggested that tourist attractions are signs . . . Sightseers do not, in any empirical sense, *see* San Francisco. They see Fisherman's Wharf, a cable car, the Golden Gate Bridge, Union Square, Coit Tower, the Presidio, City Lights Bookstore, Chinatown, and perhaps the Haight Ashbury or a nude go-go dancer in a North Beach-Barbary Coast club.

Dean MacCannell, *The Tourist: A New Theory
of the Leisure Class,* 1976: 109-111

Metaphor is pervasive in everyday life, not just in language but in thought and action. Our ordinary conceptual system, in terms of which both think and act, is fundamentally metaphoric in nature.

The concepts that govern our thought are not just matters of the intellect. They also govern our everyday functioning, down to the most mundane details. Our concepts structure what we perceive, how we get around in the world, and how we relate to other people. Our conceptual system thus plays a central role in defining our everyday realities. If we are right in suggesting that our conceptual system is largely metaphorical, then the way we think, what we experience, and what we do every day is very much a matter of metaphor.

George Lakoff and Mark Johnson,
Metaphors We Live By, 1980: 3

Chapter 5

A Primer on the Semiotics of Tourism

Semiotics is defined as the science of signs—a sign being anything that can be used to stand for something else. There are two founding fathers of the science, the Swiss linguist Ferdinand de Saussure and the American philosopher Charles Sanders Peirce.

SAUSSURE ON SIGNS

Saussure explained that signs are composed of two parts: a *signifier* (sound or object) and a *signified* (concept). He wrote:

> I propose to retain the word sign [*signe*] to designate the whole and to replace concept and sound-image respectively by *signified [signifié]* and *signifier [signifiant]*; the last two terms have the advantage of indicating the opposition that separates them from each other and from the whole of which they are parts. (1966: 67)

It is important to recognize that the relationship between signifiers and signifieds is arbitrary—that is, it is based on convention.

Saussure wrote the following, in his book *Course on General Linguistics:*

> Language is a system of signs that express ideas, and is therefore comparable to a system of writing, the alphabet of deaf-mutes, symbolic rites, polite formulas, military signals, etc. But it is the most important of these systems.

Thailand Tourism
© 2007 by The Haworth Press, Inc. All rights reserved.
doi:10.1300/5789_05

> *A science that studies the life of signs within society* is conceivable; it would be a part of social psychology and consequently of general psychology. I shall call it *semiology* (from Greek *semeion* "sign"). Semiology would show what constitutes signs, what laws govern them. (1966: 16)

Saussure called his science semiology—literally "words about signs," but that term has now been replaced by the term semiotics.

Saussure offered another important insight. Concepts, he explained, have meaning because of the web of relationships in which they are found; they do not mean anything by themselves. He wrote [my italics], *"concepts are purely differential and defined not by their positive content but negatively by their relations with the other terms of the system"* (1966: 117). He added that *"the most precise characteristics"* of these concepts *"is in being what the others are not"* (1966: 117). We find, then, that it is not content, per se, that determines meaning but *relationships* among the elements in a system. The way we make sense of concepts is by seeing them as the opposite of something else. For Saussure, then, the meanings of signs have to be learned.

PEIRCE'S SEMIOTICS:
ICONS, INDEXES, AND SYMBOLS

Charles Sanders Peirce is the other founding father of semiotics, and the one who gave the science its name. Peirce claimed that there were three kinds of signs: *icons,* which communicate by resemblance; *indexes,* which communicate by cause and effect; and *symbols,* which have to be learned. Table 5.1 shows these three kinds of signs:

There is a difference, then, between Saussure's and Peirce's ideas about signs. Peirce theorizes that only symbols are conventional and thus have to be learned. He once said, "The universe is perfused with signs, it is not composed exclusively of signs."

It makes sense, I suggest, to combine Saussure and Peirce, and suggest that we find meaning in the world by seeing everything as either a signifier of something else (a signified—that is, concept or

TABLE 5.1. Peirce's Trichotomy.

Kind:	Icon	Index	Symbol
Signify by:	Resemblance	Cause/effect	Convention
Examples:	Photographs	Fire/smoke	Flags
Process:	Can see	Can figure out	Must be taught

Source: Berger (2004).

idea) or as a sign generating meaning by being iconic, indexical, or symbolic in nature.

My analysis of Thailand's signs, which follows, is an example of what might be called sociocultural semiotics, which involves using semiotics to analyze material culture and rituals and relate these phenomena to the society in which they are found and the cultural codes operating in that society. Signs are slippery and can have many meanings. They can be used to lie, too, as the Italian semiotician Umberto Eco has explained. If a sign can be used to convey meaning, he argues, it can also be used to lie—so signs always have a double valence.

ROLAND BARTHES'S EMPIRE OF SIGNS

In his book *Empire of Signs,* a semiotic analysis of Japanese culture, the French semiotician Roland Barthes writes:

> If I want to imagine a fictive nation, I can give it an invented name, treat it declaratively as a novelistic object, create a new Garabagne, so as to compromise no real country by my fantasy (though it is then that fantasy itself I compromise by the signs of literature). I can also—though in no way claiming to represent or analyze reality itself (these being the major gestures of Western discourse)—isolate somewhere in the world *(faraway)* a certain number of features (a term employed in linguistics), and out of these features deliberately form a system. It is this system which I shall call: Japan. (1982: 3)

He adds that this system he is studying—that is, Japanese signs—is one that is "altogether detached" from his own culture. He is not, he tells us, attempting to "photograph" Japan, by which he means he will not be offering a systematic study of Japanese culture and society, but, instead, he will consider and analyze the "flashes" that Japan has offered him. Thus, he has chapters on such topics as the Japanese language, Japanese food, Tempura, Pachinko, Bowing, Japanese packages, stationery stores, Haiku, and that kind of thing. These are the kinds of things that most tourists find charming, different, interesting, and that help explain why Japan is such a fascinating country for Westerners.

From my perspective, *Empire of Signs* is a pioneering effort in the sociosemiotics of tourism and cultural analysis and I have used it as a model in analyzing Thai culture, dealing with a number of topics that were "flashes" for me when I visited the country and which I think help explain what tourists in Thailand find so interesting and intriguing. And like Barthes I come to my analysis of Thailand as a stranger, a person who has to rely on his knowledge of semiotic techniques of analysis to help make sense of this country—that, as Barthes would put it, from a touristic perspective is "a collection of important signs that we shall call Thailand."

The notions that "Thailand is paradise" or that "the islands off the coast of Thailand are little paradises" are metaphors that shape our perception of the country and our expectations of what we will find when we get there. Much of our thinking is based on metaphors—analogies that we are familiar with, and with metonymies—associations that we learn which also shape the way we interpret things. Our minds work, to a large degree, by seeing the world in terms of metaphors and metonymies—that is, analogies and associations.

As Dean MacCannell has pointed out, in the passage that begins this chapter, tourists in San Francisco do not see the city as an entity but only certain disconnected signs. In the same light, tourists in Thailand do not see Thailand as a whole but notice the way Thais smile, see beaches on Ko Samui, eat Thai food, see gold Buddhas, visit *wats,* ride in *tuk-tuks,* and that kind of thing. That is their Thailand and that is the Thailand I will be interpreting.

Rice fields and palm trees

A painting with numerous Buddhas

A beautiful plant in a temple courtyard

Tourists taking a carriage ride

Two Buddhas in a temple

A Buddha recently built in the Golden Triangle in Thailand

Thais use long sticks to hold up trees
as a sign of religious spirit

A hill tribe girl enjoys an ice cream

Thai snacks

A Thai market

A Thai crafts worker

A monk poses in Thailand

Dancers entertain tourists

A dancer at a show

A dancer at a hill tribe concert in Thailand

Tribal women dancing

An elephant artist at work

Final product

Flowers painted by an elephant in Thailand

A long-necked woman and her daughter

Chapter 6

Signs and Symbols in Thailand

In this chapter I offer a sociosemiotic analysis of a number of important signs, symbols, and other aspects of Thai culture, which tourists will generally encounter during their visits to Thailand.

THE THAI SMILE

Much has been written about the famous Thai smile. Most tourist guides say something about it, but the Thai smile is rather enigmatic, for if Thais smile at everything, its conventional meaning as something indicating pleasure, friendliness, and amusement is not adequate. From a semiotic point of view, smiles are complex signs that can mean many different things (see Exhibit 6.1).

The Semiotics of the Smile

Paul Ekman, a psychologist who has done pioneering work on facial expression, distinguishes between spontaneous and forced smiles. He calls the spontaneous smile the "Duchenne smile," tying it to the work of a French neurologist who studied the way the muscles of the face work. A forced smile involves, Ekman says, flexing a muscle called the zygomatic major that reaches from a person's cheekbone to the corner of that person's lips. With spontaneous smiles, on the other hand, there is also the flexing of small muscles around the eye, which cannot be commanded by a person. It would seem that a good deal of time, the Thai smile is a forced smile rather than a spontaneous one. But not always.

Thailand Tourism
© 2007 by The Haworth Press, Inc. All rights reserved.
doi:10.1300/5789_06

EXHIBIT 6.1. Thai smiles

Foreigners usually know Thailand first from travel brochures which often portray Thailand as the "Land of Smiles." Moreover, when visitors arrive at the airport, before they clear immigration they will see a welcome sign—a Thai lady with a smiling face, making a greeting gesture, the *"wai."* All those advertisements become real once you visit Thailand, because you will notice that smiling is the most prominent feature of the Thai character. When you arrive in Thailand, the first thing you will see from both Thai men and women is a smile. It is a part of Thai culture to greet visitors with the wai and a smile.

It may be the influence of Buddhism that makes Thai people very relaxed and easygoing. The Thais are cheerful, playful and fun-loving people. Most Thais believe that being too serious is a negative characteristic, which is why they are kind and friendly to others, particularly their guests, or even strangers.

Source: http8://www.prd.go.th/ebook/focus_thailand/v_detail1.php?focusid=171; accessed November 23, 2004.

In their book *Thailand's Turn: Profile of a New Dragon,* Elliot Kulick and Dick Wilson mention that an American journalist, Stanley Karnow, was banished from Thailand for writing that Thais "smile like Cheshire cats." They add:

> The impression of the Thai smile remains similarly vivid even after the smiler has gone. Yet a Western professor of Thai studies openly rejoiced on leaving Thailand for the last time, knowing that he would never again be irritated by that unfailing simper. The Thai smile is not just for good news or delight; it comes into play when anger, doubt, anxiety or grief are the underlying emotions, and a foreigner can easily misinterpret it.
>
> Smiling is an integral part of the Thai personality—part of the old traditional culture which is gradually altering, but is still significant in Thai life. (1992: 65)

They argue that there are three layers of Thai culture. The first and largest layer, the "traditional bottom" layer, is found mainly in rural areas and small towns and is the most difficult for foreigners to understand. The middle layer involves modernized urban Thai life, since it adapts to urban life as it exists all over the world. And the third or top layer, and the easiest for Western people to understand, involves the behavior of middle-class and upper-class people who follow Western customs.

Different Kinds of Thai Smiles

Henry Holmes and Suchanda Tangtongtavy offer a typology of different Thai smiles in their book *Working with the Thais*. I have slightly modified their list in the interest of readability.

> *Yim than nam laa:* I'm so happy I'm crying smile
> *Yim thak thaai:* The polite smile to someone you barely know
> *Yim cheun chom:* I admire you smile
> *Fuen yim:* The stiff smile–the "I should laugh at the joke though it's not funny" smile
> *Yim mee lessanai:* The smile masking something wicked in mind
> *Yik yaw:* The teasing or "I told you so" smile
> *Yim sao:* The sad smile
> *Yim haeng:* The dry smile or "I know I owe you money but don't have it" smile
> *Yim thak thaan:* I disagree with you but go ahead and propose your bad idea smile
> *Yim cheua-cheuan:* I am the winner smile, given to a losing competitor
> *Yim soo:* The smile in the face of an impossible struggle smile
> *Him mai awk:* The "I'm trying to smile but can't" smile

What this list suggests is that smiles in Thailand can mean anything and that Thais smile as a means of not signaling how they really feel. The smile is a mask that Thais use to prevent others from knowing what they think or what their emotional reaction to an event is. The Thai smile is similar to the blank face of poker players, who wish to avoid "tells," which are facial expressions and body language that reveal things about a player's cards or intentions.

Psychoanalytic Interpretation of the Thai Smile

The continual smiling of Thais is a culturally learned means of not giving away emotions, which often leads to a kind of emotional constriction and repression of feelings in many Thais. This might help explain why there is so much violence in Thai culture. What happens, it can be surmised, is that as a result of the continual repression of emotions and the Thais' inability or unwillingness to express emotion, their anger and frustration build up to dangerous levels and then explode, when something sets them off.

The smile is, in many cases, a kind of inhibitor of emotions and would imply that many Thais feel lonely and isolated. This feeling may be connected to the sense of independence found in Thais and the notion that they do not think in terms of social and cultural responsibilities but rather in terms of their circle of families and friends. Responsibility radiates outward from the core family. So the smile would be connected, in many cases, to a sense of rage and to a diffused hostility that hides behind the Thai mask of affability. That may explain why there is so much violence in Thai society, as reflected in the statistics on murder in Thailand, discussed earlier.

KING BHUMIBOL ADULYADEJ OF THAILAND

The story of Thailand, until 1932, is the story of Thai kings. In his history of Thailand, David K. Wyatt writes that he has not spent much time dealing with peasant farmers in Thailand, who remain more or less in the shade in his book, but that "Kings, on the other hand, are on nearly every page" (1984: xiv). This is because until the absolute monarchy in Thailand ended, royal reigns were real units of time. Individual rulers, he explains, had enormous power over the lives of their subjects. He adds that readers interested in the history of Thailand expect to read a great deal about kings, since they were so important. After 1932, when a military junta seized control of the government, the military started playing a more important role in Thai life, a role that continues to this day.

The Royal Kingdom of Thailand

We forget that Thailand is a royal kingdom, and Bhumibol (spelled many different ways in English), the Thai king, is held in great respect. It is considered an insult not to rise when the national anthem or the royal anthem is played. The royal anthem is played before films begin in movie theaters and patrons in these theaters always rise, to honor their king.

The king reigns but does not rule, since Thailand is a constitutional monarchy. He has great moral power and is held in reverence by Thais, some of whom consider him to be a sacred personage. Bhumibol has had to be extremely adroit in not asserting himself too much and irritating the various rulers, both civilian and military, who make the most important decisions in Thailand. Between 1923 and 1997, Thailand has had sixteen different constitutions, the last one being passed in 1997. And governments come and go with remarkable speed. Somehow, Thailand holds together—probably because of the core of civil servants who deal with the economy and because of the sobering presence of the king.

The first important modern Thai king was Chulalongkorn, who reigned from 1868 to 1910, and is reputed to have had seventy-six children—his first when he was only fourteen years old. And Chulalongkorn's father, King Mongkut, is reputed to have had eighty-two children. He reigned from 1851 to 1868 and was responsible for helping Thailand to modernize. He was the king in the film "Anna and the King of Siam," although the events in that film are sheer fantasy. Chulalongkorn's son Vajiravudh reigned from 1910 to 1925 and he was succeeded by Prajadhikpok, who reigned from 1925 to 1935. He was succeeded by his son, Ananda.

When Ananda died, from a mysterious bullet to his head, Bhumibol, his younger brother, became king, at the age of 18. Table 6.1 lists the kings I have discussed, all from the Chakri dynasty, and the periods in which they reigned.

TABLE 6.1. Kings of Thailand.

King	Period of reign
Mongkut	April 3, 1851 to October 1, 1868
Chulalongkorn	October 1, 1868 to October 23, 1910
Vajiravudh	October 23, 1910 to November 26, 1925
Prajadhikpok	November 26, 1925 to March 2, 1935 (abdicated)
Ananda	March 2, 1935 to June 9, 1946
Bhumibol	June 9, 1946 to present

Source: Author's compilation.

We can say that Bhumibol is an accidental king, a person who never expected to become king.

A Source of Stability in a Chaotic Country

At first, King Bhumibol cultivated an image of himself as an amiable but not particularly serious person, and was often shown on television playing the saxophone with jazz bands. That was to disarm those who might resent him being on the throne and, possibly, threatening their power. He also spent several weeks as a monk, in the Thai tradition. Over the years, however, as the Thai people showed their love for him, and started thinking about him as semidivine, he assumed more and more power in the moral sphere and now is enormously influential. In 1987, some 40 million people in Thailand signed a petition to add "The Great" to his title and now he reigns as Bhumibol The Great.

He is, it turns out, the longest reigning monarch in the world at the present time. And he has functioned to provide an enormous amount of stability to Thai culture and society, a center to a country where the individualistic Thais might fly off in many different directions were he not there to provide some guidance. King Bhumibol is, in a sense, above politics—though he does make his wishes known at critical moments. A 1992 photograph of the king seated, while a Thai general was on his knees before the king, is a telling comment on the power of this king.

It also should be noted that King Bhumibol is one of the wealthiest men in Thailand, controlling the Siam Commercial Bank and the Siam Cement Corporation. The king's Crown Properties Bureau owns an enormous amount of land and has investments in forty companies. It was estimated, as of 1992, to be "the second largest asset holder and fourth-largest investor in the kingdom" (Kulick and Wilson, 1992: 54-55).

Stalin once asked, "How many divisions has the Pope?" King Bhumibol may have no divisions, but he has sixty million Thais behind him and a great deal of wealth, and the generals and civil servants who run the country are well aware of that fact.

Thai bill with King Bhumibol's likeness

BANGKOK, "CITY OF ANGELS"

Bangkok provides the first taste of Thailand for most international visitors and it is quite a remarkable introduction to Thailand. Many Thais consider Bangkok to represent the "essence" of Thailand, and it may be quintessentially Thai, but it also is quite different, in scale and ambience, from most other Thai cities.

Bangkok: The Dominant City in Thailand

Bangkok is the financial and cultural center of Thailand, a gigantic agglomeration (defined as a main city and neighborhood communities) of 7.5 million people—some say 10 million people is more accurate—whose traffic jams are of awesome proportions and whose smog is a danger to ordinary people and life threatening to people with asthma and other respiratory problems. There are several million vehicles in Bangkok that pump an estimated metric ton of lead as well as other toxic matter into the air every year. The Chao Phraya River, which runs through Bangkok, is terribly contaminated. Bangkok is built on the delta of this river, which often floods, and is slowly sinking into the delta, at an estimated rate of an inch per year. So the city faces incredible problems.

According to Gaunt Milieu (1991), Bangkok covers 600 square miles, which means its area is approximately 20 miles by 30 miles. It is at least ten times as large as the next largest city in Thailand, Chiang Mai. Some 90 percent of all motor vehicles in Thailand are registered in Bangkok; it contains most of the government offices as well as the residences of the king and the Supreme Patriarch of the Buddhist faith.

But Bangkok is, it turns out, only thirty-second on the list of urban agglomerations, far behind the largest agglomeration, Tokyo, with 33.9 million people, the second largest, Mexico City, with 22.1 million people, and the third largest, Seoul, with 21.9 million people.

Bangkok As a Center for Thai In-Migration

The Thais in the countryside, like people in many countries in the developing world, look toward Bangkok as a place to go to find jobs, and their continual movement to the city has put incredible strains on it in terms of public services and housing, among other things. It has huge slums full of people looking for jobs or barely getting by and, it is estimated, to have hundreds of thousands of prostitutes, catering to the desires of sex tourists and of the Thais, as well.

Approximately one in every eight people in Thailand lives in Bangkok and its surrounding areas and most international tourists who come to Thailand do so by flying into Bangkok. Those on package tours generally remain in Bangkok for a day or two, to see the main tourist attractions: the Grand Palace, Wat Arum, Wat Phra, rides on the river and similar kinds of sights, and then move off—either to the north, on cultural tours, or to the south, where there are beautiful beaches and for some, the classic trio: sea, sand, and sex.

Bangkok can be described as one gigantic traffic jam with buildings in between the buses, cars, trucks, *tuk-tuks,* and other vehicles. The new skyway system helps a great deal but getting around Bangkok is a daunting task. On the other hand, Bangkok has its charms and despite the pollution, chaotic traffic, and other problems, many tourists find, to their surprise, that they like the city. And that is because it is a rather fantastic city, with remarkable *wats* (temples) and other important tourist sites, an endless number of bars, hip restaurants, and thousands of small restaurants where some excellent food is served. In short, Bangkok is a bit of a surprise and there is plenty to do and see in the few days, which is the amount of time most tourists give Bangkok.

Bangkok's real name is eighteen words long in Thai *(Krungthep mahanakorn amorn ratthanakosin mahinthara ayutthaya mahadilok phoppthananphrat ratchathani burirom udomratchaniwet mahasathan amornphiman awattornsatitit sakka phathorn wisanu kammarasit)* but it is generally known as *krungthep*, "city of angels." It is described by many Thais as *khwaam pen thai*—the essence or epitome of Thai-ness. So Bangkok gives tourists who visit the city a heightened and concentrated sense of what they might expect when they move on to the smaller cities in the north or the beach towns in the south, where tourists will experience Thai culture but in a generally more leisurely, somewhat diluted, and easier to breathe form.

THE BUDDHIST MONKS OF THAILAND

The early morning procession of saffron-robed Buddhist monks, out with their "begging" bowls (as some books put it), receiving food from the Thai people, is one of the more colorful and significant scenes from Thai life. The monks have shaved heads and eyebrows, and move in an orderly procession, through the streets of the communities where they live. Thais believe that giving food to monks is the means for getting merits, which will be of importance to them—in their present lives and future ones. The monks are followers of Theravada Buddhism and Thailand is the second largest Theravada Buddhist country, trailing Japan in this matter.

The Lifestyle of Buddhist Monks

Their lifestyle is generally speaking ascetic—they do not eat after noon—and they are sworn to celibacy, which explains, in part, why women cannot touch them. If a woman, by chance, touches a monk, he must undergo a complicated purification ritual. This implies that women are "unclean" and thus contact with a woman, even if it is accidental, contaminates a monk.

In more recent times, some monks have enlarged their sphere of operation and some dabble in the stock market and others have businesses. Traditionally, monks made money by officiating at weddings and the openings of businesses, telling fortunes, and so on. Some have been known to have sex with women and others have political views that the government does not like.

Monks are at the top of the social order in Thailand, even above the king. The official organization of Buddhism in Thailand is called the *sangha*. It corresponds, vaguely, to the papacy for Catholics. The *sangha* determines religious doctrine and the practices that monks and other Buddhists will follow.

The Autonomy of Monks: Laws Unto Themselves

Melford E. Spiro, an anthropologist of religion, describes the autonomy that monks feel. In his chapter "Symbolism and Functionalism in the Anthropological Study of Religion" he writes:

> The true Buddhist is the monk. The monastic community (Sangha) is an elite, consisting of those few who possess the necessary spiritual qualifications *(paramita)* to practice the Dhamma [the Buddhist teaching or law] in its entirety, including the 227 regulations that comprise the monastic rule (Vinaya). Distinguished from this elite is the great mass of laymen who are spiritually qualified to follow only the Five Precepts (to refrain from lying, killing, stealing, drunkenness, and sexual immorality). The layman can only hope that the piety exhibited in his present birth will enable him to acquire sufficient merit so that, in a future birth, he too will have the qualifications for admission to the monastic order. (1979: 328)

In Buddhism, as Spiro explains, everyone aspires then to become a monk and build up enough merits to be able to develop the spiritual qualifications to do so.

Spiro continues with a discussion of the autonomous nature of Theravada Buddhism, that shows how it contrasts with other religions. Spiro explains:

In Buddhism, neither laymen nor Sangha, whether separately or jointly, comprise a church, a corporate group. Even within the monastic order each monk (or, at any event, each monastery) is a law unto himself (or itself). This organizational feature of the Sangha parallels the ideological structure of Buddhism: each individual must seek his own salvation. As the Master stressed in a famous Sutta, monks must "wander along like the rhinoceros," or, as He put it in yet another metaphor, they must "live as islands unto [themselves]." (1979: 328)

This helps explain the character of life in Thailand and the Thai sensibility. Thais, generally speaking, do not have a social sensibility or outlook. It is Buddhism that provides Thais with their worldview, with their sense of how things work. Buddhism is a means of obtaining nirvana, an end to the continual cycle of birth and rebirth, as well as deliverance from the thirty-one realms of existence in Buddhism, and this salvation that Buddhists seek is individualistic in two senses: only individuals can be saved and individuals are responsible for saving themselves.

Monks and Modernization

This helps explain the expression one finds on the faces of the Buddhist monks one sees in Thailand—an expression that suggests both peacefulness and self-importance. I have found this same expression on the faces of many religious people. It is a sense that they have, through their faith and a knowledge beyond that of ordinary people, of the workings of the world, an enormous sense of dignity and power.

Spiro argues that the cynosure of Buddhist societies (he actually is talking about Buddhism in Burma, but his ideas apply equally to Thailand) is the monk, who has renounced the world and whose ideal is to be an *arhant,* someone who is oblivious to the suffering of others and seeks and gains salvation for himself.

It is estimated that there are 32,000 Buddhist monasteries and 460,000 Buddhist monks—most belonging to the Mahunikai sect (which outnumbers the Thammayet sect by around 35 to 1). Mahunikai monks can eat twice before noon and accept side dishes; Thammayet monks eat only once before noon.

Kulick and Wilson suggest that the institution of monkhood seems to be waning and that the custom in which Thais become monks for short periods of time also is losing popularity. What Kulick and Wilson write is that as the old traditions of monkhood are waning, new sects of monks are arising—sects that are much more societally involved. Of these monks, Kulick and Wilson write:

> Most of them turn their backs decisively on the paraphernalia of the old temple setup—fortune telling, lotteries, amulets and charms. They respect the Buddha image but not worship it. They retreat from the pointless old collective rituals and march firmly into the liberated social arena where selves cry out for cultivation. . . . These sects are the nearest counterparts of the "protestant ethic" supposedly driving some northern Europe societies. (1992: 104)

These new sects of monks are doing what sects often do—reinterpret the old ways and reinvigorate the religion. Web sites on the Internet describe the role some monks are playing in fighting AIDS, for example. Some monks become scholars and teachers; so our notions about what monks do has to be broadened considerably.

It remains to be seen whether the orange-robed monks that tourists see in Thailand are the remnants of a dying form of Buddhism or the core of the Buddhism that has room for all kinds of monks. If many monks are adapting to a changing Thai society, you might imagine that the fate of the old-fashioned monks would seem to be sealed. They will be left behind and become irrelevant. But it may be that the changes in Thai society are, actually, somewhat superficial, and the monks, as they change their mission in the world, will continue to shape Thai culture and society.

BUDDHA STATUES

It has been estimated that there are some 30,000 *wats* (temples) in Thailand, and each of these *wats* has one or more statues of Buddha. There are hundreds of thousands of other statues of Buddha scattered throughout Thailand. The guidebooks to Thailand mention some of the more important Buddha statues, such as the Emerald Buddha at

A large Buddha figure

Wat Phrae Kaeo and the five-ton, solid gold Buddha at Wat Trimitr. Some companies take tourists to a factory in Phitsanulok to see how Buddha images are manufactured. These Buddha statues are indicators of the important of Theravana Buddhism in Thailand.

Buddha Statues and Buddhism in Thailand

Thailand is a Buddhist country and the impact of Buddhism on the Thai psyche, on Thai culture, and Thai society has been, and still is, profound. The orange-robed monks one sees in the early mornings with their alms bowls are daily visual reminders of Buddhism's impact and its all-pervasive influence—of the way it informs so much of life in Thailand. The Buddha statues are there, all the time—with that enigmatic expression on their faces and their highly stylized eye designs. For Westerners, there is something puzzling about them and their impact.

The Role of Buddhism in Thai Culture

Elliott Kulick and Dick Wilson discuss the role of Buddhism in their book *Thailand's Turn: Profile of a New Dragon:*

> Buddhism was one of the bonds bringing Chinese immigrants together with Thais, but it is also an important constituent in the general success story of Thai modernization. Thailand is the second-largest Buddhist state after Japan, and the precepts of Theravada Buddhism that Thais profess explain much about their personality, old and new. Thailand's royal ceremonies, its thousands of high-roofed temples, its gaggles of monks in their orange robes and begging bowls going out for alms in the light of every dawn, the constant citation of Buddhist aphorisms by public figures all point to a national religion that runs deep— deeper, perhaps, even than Christianity in some Western countries. (1992: 97)

Buddhism, they explain, plays a major role in every aspect of Thai life—and informs Thai economic, social, political, intellectual, and cultural life. It is, they suggest, the foundation on which Thai life

Walking Buddhas

rests. And these Buddhas that one sees everywhere are permanent reminders of the power of Buddhism.

The Fundamentals of Theravada Buddhism

In his article on the anthropological study of religion, Spiro describes the fundamental beliefs found in Theravada Buddhism. He writes:

> The Buddhist Teaching, or Law (Dhamma), stresses two themes: suffering *(dukkha)* is one of the three essential attributes of sentient existence—the other two are impermanence and non-self— any attempt to change the world which is based on the assumption that suffering can thereby be eliminated is irrational. Not only can such attempts not succeed, but they have the opposite effect: they not only increase suffering by increasing attachment *(tanha)* to the world (the ultimate cause of suffering), but such attachment, in turn, precludes the attainment of nirvana, the only goal whose attainment signals the extinction of suffering. (1979: 326-327)

Buddhism, Spiro explains, involves an endless chain of births and rebirths and Buddhist law offers itself as a means of ending the wheel of life and attaining nirvana. Buddhism contains a sacred being (Buddha), a sacred law (Dhamma) that is revealed by this sacred being, and a sacred community of monks (Sangha), which lives according to the precepts of this law. For most Thais, Spiro adds, work is not valued in itself, achievement is not a goal, and individuals' concerns are held to be basic, in contrast to a focus on group values and social well-being. The Buddha does not redeem others; what he does do is teach others how to redeem themselves and his Way focuses upon renouncing the world rather than transforming it.

When Thais see these Buddha statues, the following is the message they get from them: Renounce the world rather than trying to transform it. When Westerners look at these Buddha statues, in their various formulations (gigantic Buddhas, lying Buddhas, solid gold Buddhas, emerald Buddhas), they see objects that are often very beautiful and that have a strange and enigmatic presence. Buddha was seen as a teacher and is not revered as a god, but as you gaze at

The "Talking Buddha"

these Buddhas and observe the way Thais relate to them, you cannot help feeling that these Buddha statues play a role very similar to that of Christ in his various manifestations in pictorial art and sculpture.

Thailand As a New Economic Dragon

If the ascetic, world-renouncing, monk is the Buddhist ideal and if Buddhism focuses its attention on personal salvation and passivity, how do you explain the incredible economic progress that Thailand has made in the past few decades? How does Buddhist thought, with its fatalism and belief in karma and renunciation of the world, lead to the so-called Thai economic miracle?

What seems to have happened is that many monks and revisionist Buddhist sects have adapted to modernization and even played a role in its development. The very nature of the institutionalized Buddhist religion, in which monks are "laws unto themselves," facilitates this kind of activity. And now we find Buddhist monks working on

AIDS-prevention programs, helping to feed the poor, and performing other tasks that would seem to be at odds with the official Buddhist doctrine.

It is possible to make a distinction between official Buddhist dogma and actual Buddhist practice, both in terms of the lives of monks and the lives of ordinary people. People may pay lip service to the Sangha, the official rules, and it may play an important role in many aspects of Thai culture and society, but in their everyday lives Thais drink and dance and amuse themselves like people all over the world. Indeed, the Thai people have a joyfulness and cheerfulness that makes visiting Thailand a great pleasure.

The Buddha and Reaction Formation

Sigmund Freud used the term "reaction formation" to explain the behavior of a person who might hate someone but acts lovingly toward the object of his hatred. There is a kind of reversal that takes place and we mask our feelings by acting in the opposite manner. This might be what is at work in Thai culture, where a religious notion of predestination and karma can have the effect of liberating people to be active and to live in a joyful manner.

It is also possible to interpret Buddhist doctrine in a way that would sanction being in the world, and acting in it, for the average person; we must remember that the Sangha really applies to the sacred community of monks, and even there the monks are free to interpret Buddhist theology as they wish and many monks are teachers and professors and others are involved in doing what they can to alleviate the suffering of the poor and afflicted in Thailand.

ELEPHANTS AND THE THAI PSYCHE

The elephant is the national animal of Thailand and elephants have played an important role, over the centuries, in giving Thais a national identity. It also happens that elephants have a certain symbolic significance in the United States. The elephant is the symbol of the Republican Party in America and there was a popular joke cycle about elephants in America a number of years ago.

The Symbolic Importance of Elephants in Thailand

There is a tradition in Thailand of kings having white elephants (determining whether an elephant is white is a complicated and controversial matter) and the present king of Thailand, Bhumibol, has ten white elephants. This is a sign of good luck and power. His brother, who had been king and died under mysterious circumstances, had no white elephants—the only king in recent years to be without them. Elephants are considered by Thais as symbols of a king's divine right to rule and his wisdom and power. Elephants are also believed to bring luck and they have religious significance in Buddhism as well. They are symbols of the strength of the mind of Buddha and the power of Buddhist thought. One often finds elephants in Buddhist iconology: statues, reliefs, and other works of art. The Thais even have a national elephant day, in honor of the animal, every March 13.

In a chapter titled "Classification of Animals in Thailand," S. J. Tambiah discusses the symbolic significance of elephants. His article is about the way Thais in a particular village classify animals, but it holds true for Thais, in general, I would suggest. He points out that these Thai villagers classify animals in terms of whether they are domesticated *(sad baan)* or forest animals *(sad paa)*. The elephant comes under the *sad paa* classification of "animals of the deep forest, rarely seen" and nonedible (1973: 137). After discussing domesticated animals, he writes about the symbolic significance of elephants:

> There is another class of animals of the deep forest which are considered inedible. They are the elephant, tiger, leopard, lion and bear. These animals represent to the villagers the power, danger, and might of the forest as opposed to human settlements, and they are viewed with admiration and awe and fear. Villagers hardly ever encounter them in their wild state, and hence they seem almost mythical to them. Inedibility here simply refers to their existence in a world remote from the human. All except the bear are included in the list of Buddhist food taboos. However, because of their special status, they are used for vehicles for expressing certain ideas and values. . . . The elephant stands for inherited size and strength (waasaana maag) . . .

when caught and domesticated [it] becomes a royal animal and
is then an animal useful to man. (145-146)

Of all the wild and powerful animals of the deep forest, only the elephant can be domesticated. Thus, it has an ambivalent role in the Thai
imagination: it is both a wild animal and one that can be domesticated.

At one time, many years ago, there were an estimated 100,000 elephants in Thailand; now there are thought to be only 1,500 wild elephants and perhaps a few thousand domesticated ones. They are the
largest land animal, possessed of enormous strength, and it is this
strength and power, and their wildness, that makes them so important
in the Thai imagination. Traditionally elephants were "broken" by
being deprived of sleep, water, and food and by being beaten while
confined in small wooden confines—what are called "crushes." In recent years, there is a new theory of elephant training that has become
popular and some elephants are being trained in a much more hu-
mane manner—much the way we train dogs—by positive reinforce-
ment. The elephants are rewarded by being given food when they do
things their mahouts (trainers) want them to do and gradually learn
how to do what is expected of them.

Thais often say that Thailand is shaped like an elephant, with the
head representing most of the country and the long, thin southern part
of the country representing the elephant's trunk. This suggests that,
psychologically speaking, the Thais live in what might be described
as a nationally symbolic elephant of a country that plays a role in
shaping their character and psyche.

The Elephant in Modern Thailand

The elephant in Thailand is, symbolically, a link between the modern Thais, living in the vast urban conglomeration of Bangkok or
smaller cities and villages, and the mythic past of Thailand, as a primitive natural paradise, a land of the deep forest. Over the years, as the
population of Thailand has grown, wild elephants have lost much of
their habitat and now find themselves in a desperate situation. (In the
United States we face the same problem with bears and wolves, who
return us, psychically, to our earlier days in the frontier, which is seen
as an American natural paradise.) The 1,500 or so trained and domes-

ticated elephants find themselves with little work to do, now that Thailand has banned logging. They were used, when logging was allowed, to move huge logs, as a natural kind of bulldozer.

Ironically, it is the tourism industry that has come to the rescue of the Thai elephants. Many tourists in Thailand take elephant rides as part of their tours and so a number of elephants survive by giving tourists rides. And some elephants, in a rather bizarre turn of events, have been given paint brushes to paint, and now function as primitive artists, creating paintings that have found a market in Thailand and elsewhere. A number of urban elephants make their living, so to speak, by being used to sell various products, by lending their symbolic weight to weddings and other life-cycle events, where having an elephant in attendance is thought to bring good luck. It is a precarious and difficult existence for these urban elephants.

Elephants bathing in a river with a mahout

The Thai Elephant and the Thai Husband: A Psychoanalytic Hypothesis

One can only wonder whether the domesticated elephant in Thailand also symbolizes the changes that have taken place in the Thai male in recent years? He too, if the portrayal of marital relations in Thai comic books is accurate, has been domesticated and weakened.

Marriage for Thai men, it would seem, represents a process similar to what happens to elephants in their "crushes." The male Thai, by upbringing a highly individualistic "law unto himself," finds himself, when he gets married, confined in apartments and houses and tied down, if not crushed, by the burdens of family life and a now domineering mahout-like wife. For the downtrodden Thai husband, the elephant provides a symbolic release and returns the male, in his fantasies and dreams, to his days as a wild bachelor, as a figure of power and significance.

ETHNIC TRIBES

Almost every "classic" tour of Thailand takes tourists to visit with ethnic tribes in the hills in the northern part of the country. It is estimated that there are about 500,000 tribal people in Thailand, of whom the Yang or Kariang, with about 320,000 people, are the most numerous. Thais call these ethnic tribes mountain people, or chao khao. Except for the Yang, the ethnic tribes are seminomadic in origin, and have come to Thailand from neighboring countries, such as China, Tibet, Laos, and Burma.

Time Travel

Why do these people fascinate us so much? Let me offer a hypothesis that might explain the matter. Many of these ethnic tribal people live, and dress, the way they have done for hundreds of years—especially the women, in their often elaborate native costumes. Thus, when tourists from modern societies visit these tribes, as part of their cultural tours, they are, in essence, time traveling—backward hundreds of years to see how people lived in those days. They are playing the role, in a diluted way, of the great travelers and explorers of earlier times when travel had a certain aura of excitement about it.

In his book *Tristes Tropics: An Anthropological Study of Primitive Societies in Brazil,* Claude Lévi-Strauss writes:

> I should have liked to live in the age of *real* travel, when the spectacle on offer had not yet been blemished, contaminated, and confounded; then I could have seen Lahore not as I saw it, but as it appeared to Bernier, Tavernier, Manucci. . . . There's no end, of course, to such conjectures. When was the right moment to see India? At what period would the study of the Brazilian savage have yielded the purest satisfaction and the savage himself have been at his peak? . . . The alternative is inescapable: either I am a traveller in ancient times, and faced with a prodigious spectacle which would be almost entirely unintelligible to me and might, indeed, provoke me to mockery or disgust; or I am a traveller of our own day, hastening in search of a vanished reality. (1970: 44-45)

What tourists who visit ethnic tribes in Thailand do is find remnants of this "vanished reality" that Lévi-Strauss talks about. He argues that once there was such a thing as "real" travel, which it turns out was done mostly by elites or well-financed explorers, before travel had been corrupted by all the package deals found in modern-day mass tourism.

The Search for Authenticity

Many scholars who study tourism suggest that tourists are in search of "authenticity" in contrast to the staged and artificial experiences and "pseudo-events" to which they often are exposed. Tourists, it is suggested, want to see life as it really is lived and want to avoid fake or ersatz experiences. Tourists want to avoid "tourist traps" and similar frauds.

Visiting ethnic tribes is an attempt to see how these people from the "fourth world" live and a means of satisfying our curiosity about the incredibly varied ways in which people organize their lives. Visiting ethnic tribes in Thailand throws our own lives into sharp relief. Members of these tribes find themselves in a difficult situation nowadays. If they assimilate into Thai society at large, they lose—or certainly dilute—their identities, but if they remain the way they are, they seem destined to live in poverty. Most of the members of these tribes are not citizens, cannot own land, and do not have access to schooling or health care. So when tourists come to visit these tribes, who are often living, more or less, the way they did hundreds of years ago, the members of the ethnic tribes become time-travelers as well—but forward, into the future. They can see what the future—that is, the world of the twenty-first century—is like.

Ironically, it probably is the case that the development of tourism to the various ethnic minorities in Thailand (and in other countries as well) has the effect of strengthening their cultural identities, since these identities and the "otherness" of the ethnic tribes are what brings tourists to visit these people and thus are a source of income for them. So, curiously, tourism may be playing an important role in helping ethnic minorities maintain, to some degree, their cultural identities. Tourism also has implications in terms of making the Thai government aware of the economic benefits of having these hill tribal people and doing something about such matters as infrastructure, education, and health care for them. Furthermore, tourism may also cause leading members of these ethnic tribes to make certain changes in the way they live and present themselves to tourists, to make themselves a better "sell" to tourists and provide, for example, better photo opportunities.

In his book, *The Commercialized Crafts of Thailand: Hill Tribes and Lowland Villages,* Erik Cohen suggests that notions many people have about the impact of tourism and modernity on third- and fourth-world people are incorrect. The image many people have of tourism and modernity necessarily leading to "inauthentic" crafts from Thai craftsmen is wrong, Cohen says, since it neglects that fact that long before Western tourism arrived in Thailand, the Thai crafts workers had been affected by globalization and had commercialized their products, to varying degrees. In recent years, the impact of tourism and other forces has been considerable, however. But this doesn't mean that the Thai artisans will abandon their traditional arts. As Cohen explains:

> It should be noted indeed that even in the past most Third and Fourth world people were not isolated from external influences. Their arts and crafts were throughout history influenced by the

styles, designs, materials and techniques of other cultures and societies, even as they influenced them. It is true, however, that in recent times such influences have been extraordinarily intrusive and often destructive at least in the short run. (2000: 5)

One reason we might assume that tourism and other forces have impacted, if not destroyed, traditional arts and crafts in Thailand is that we took an ahistorical perspective. We assumed that members of Thai hill tribes and lowland villages were, somehow, living in a state of nature and radical innocence and were not affected by historical forces, and thus succumbed, easily, to the impact of tourism and other forces tied to modernity. This idea, Cohen suggests, is mistaken. We should keep Cohen's insights in mind when we think about—and read about—the relationship that exists between tourists and members of the so-called native or traditional cultures.

In his new book, *Very Thai: Everyday Popular Culture,* Philip Cornwel-Smith, explains, "In one dizzying spasm, Thailand is experiencing the forces that took a century to transform the West" (2005: 47). Andrew Marshall, who reviewed the book in *Time* magazine explains that Thai-ness has become "whatever tourists want" (2005: 47). Yet Thailand remains, Marshall adds, an enigmatic combination of the modern and the traditional, of all kinds of opposites, where, as Cornwel-Smith put it, "the principal rite is the right to shop" (*Time,* 2005: 47).

The Tourist Gaze

The English sociologist John Urry has written a book titled *The Tourist Gaze.* In his essay "Globalizing the Tourist Gaze," he suggests that tourists consume signs and symbols (which can be photographed or videotaped) when they travel, and that tourism privileges the eye rather than other senses. Urry focuses on the global dimensions of the tourist gaze and writes:

There has been a massive shift from a more of less single tourist gaze in the nineteenth century to a proliferation of countless discourses, forms and embodiments of tourist gazes now. In a simple sense we can talk of the globalizing of the tourist gaze, as multiple gazes have become core to global culture sweeping almost

everywhere in their awesome wake . . . Tourism has become mas-
sively mediatised, while everyday sites of activity get re-designed
in "tourist" mode, as with many themed environments.

As tourism has become a mass phenomenon, spreading all over the
world, the tourist gaze, the most important element in tourism as Urry
sees things, has then become globalized, as well.

There is some question about whether tourism can be restricted so
much to the visual gaze. It is assumed, of course, that the tourist-
gazer is a dominant figure and the people who are gazed at, often in
postcolonial and third-world countries, are in a weakened position.
Thailand, we must remember, was never a colony; so it remains a
special case. Some theorists liken tourism to what might be described
as "soft imperialism," in which people from dominant first-world societies travel to other cultures to amuse and entertain themselves,
reliving the imperialism experience in a modernized and more sani-
tized form.

Mary Louise Pratt writes:

Social spaces where disparate cultures meet, clash, and grapple
with each other, often in highly asymmetrical relations of domination and subordination—like colonialism, slavery, or the af-
termaths as they are lived out across the globe today. (1992)

She calls these spaces "contact zones," a term that has become very
popular with writers about tourism, since it offers a rather graphic image of tourists and peoples they encounter in their travels.

She describes contact zones as:

The space of colonial encounters, the space in which peoples
geographically and historically separated come into contact
with each other and establish ongoing relationships, usually involving conditions of coercion, radical inequality, and intractable
conflict. (http://www.social.schass.ncsu.edu/wyrick/debclass/
gtprat.htm)

This involves, among other things, travelers and the objects of their
interest and gazes, "travelees."

When tourists visit ethnic tribes in Thailand, they are looking not
only for authenticity but also for insights into the human condition

and human variability and also insights into their own lives. That is what the "otherness" found in these ethnic tribes signifies. We make sense of the world, we find meaning in the world, by noting differences. Saussure, the great Swiss linguist, said that in language there are only differences—which help us understand what words mean—and the same applies to the way we find meaning in the world.

The question is, then—Are tourists in Thailand, who visit these ethnic people, exploiting them and might the impact of tourism lead to members of these people deciding to assimilate into Thai culture? It can be argued that the visits by the tourists have led to these people strengthening their traditions since it is their radical otherness that brings tourists to them and enables these tribal people to earn income. These ethnic people may even enhance their performances as objects of tourist curiosity, a phenomenon that Dean MacCannell calls "staged authenticity" in his book *The Tourist: A New Theory of the Leisure Class.* This staged authenticity involves a performance, of sorts, put on by those being visited, to satisfy the notions tourists have learned from advertising and tourist guidebooks about what they will be seeing.

There is reason to suggest that the notion of the tourist gaze is simplistic and too one-dimensional. Gaze theorists do not take into account what might be described as the return gaze, by people who are being gazed at by tourists. In addition, gaze theorists do not consider the fact that there is often considerable interaction between tourists and people in the countries these tourists are visiting. So while it seems evident that there is an important visual dimension to tourism, which involves "the tourist gaze" and the photography and videotaping that often accompany this gaze, the relationship between gazers and those being gazed at is often more complicated than gaze theorists admit.

The Hill Tribes and the Exotic

One of the things many tourists seek is what might be described as "the exotic," which involves such things as being remote, different, and unusual, among other things. European countries such as France and Italy are different from the United States, but they are not exotic. Thailand, and many other countries in Southeast Asia, are seen by tourists as exotic. When tourists visit ethnic tribes, and see women with numerous rings around their necks or women in strange costumes, they categorize such things as exotic. In Table 6.2 I offer a comparison between everyday life and the exotic.

TABLE 6.2. Everyday life and the exotic.

Everyday life	The exotic
Near	Distant
The present	The past
Familiar	Strange
Modern	Ancient, traditional
The skyscraper	The hut
The supermarket	The souk
Cathedrals	Hindu temples, mosques
Euro-American cuisine	Ethnic cuisines
Electronic	Mechanical
Suits, dresses	Turbans, robes, costumes

Source: Berger (2003).

Table 6.2 draws upon my analysis of the exotic in my book *Deconstructing Travel: Cultural Perspectives on Tourism.*

It is the otherness of the hill tribes that makes them exotic. They are far removed, in the way they live, even from most people in the third world and thus they fascinate us, since their existence suggests an entirely different outlook on life and way of organizing society. As I suggested earlier, through the ethnic tribes in the hills of Thailand, we can engage in a kind of time-travel, hundreds of years back, when the only travelers who interacted with such people were explorers and adventurers. Now this experience is open to tourists of all kinds and we all can become cultural anthropologists, of sorts.

We learn from our travels. Paul Fussell, in a book he edited, *The Norton Book of Travel,* explains that travel:

> . . . conveys the pleasure of learning new things, and as Aristotle observed over 2,300 years ago, not only philosophers but people in general like learning things, even if the learning comes disguised as "entertainment." It is as learners that explorers, tourists, and genuine travelers, otherwise so different in motives and behavior, come together. Explorers learn the contours of undiscovered shorelines and mountains, tourists learn exchange rates and where to go in Paris for the best hamburgers. . . . Travelers

learn not just foreign customs and curious cuisines and unfamiliar beliefs and novel forms of government. They learn, if they are lucky, humility. Experiencing on their senses a world different from their own, they realize their provincialism and recognize their ignorance. (1987: 13,14)

So one benefit of travel and of experiencing the exotic is that we learn to be more humble and recognize that there are many different interesting cultures to be explored and different ways of organizing societies.

WATS *(TEMPLES)*

To visit Thailand is to visit numerous *wats,* to explore them, and to admire the Buddha figures and other statues they contain. If travel in Europe involves castles and cathedrals, travel in Thailand involves visiting different *wats*—especially ones of historic or artistic importance. There are an estimated 30,000 *wats* in Thailand and these *wats,* with their tall stupas and richly ornamented design, help give the Thai landscape its charm and distinctiveness.

The Design of Wats

It is best to think of *wats* as compounds, containing a number of different buildings. They are not unitary edifices, like churches and cathedrals, though they often contain buildings that house priests and ministers and sometimes school. Perhaps monastery is the most apt description of *wats.* The most important part of a *wat* is the *ubosoth,* which is where religious services are held. Second in importance is the place where Buddhists assemble—to give food to the monks, attend sermons, or pray.

There are also, generally speaking, a number of buildings that house monks. One of the most outstanding parts of the *wats* are the *cheddis* or stupas, the tall pagodas that house sacred relics. These stupas often dominate the skylines in smaller cities and towns in Thailand.

Wats are generally full of statues of the Buddha and other religious figures; often they contain statues of elephants, and beautiful religious murals. Some contain footprints of the Buddha. *Wats* tend to be very decorative and elaborate and quite eclectic in terms of the styles of art they contain. Some of the *wats* are famous, such as Wat Trimtr, which houses a solid gold statue of Buddha (reputedly the largest solid gold statue, weighing five tons, in the world), Wat Po, with the giant 150 foot long "reclining Buddha," and Wat Phra Kaeo, which houses a famous emerald Buddha. All of these *wats* are in Bangkok, but there are other important *wats* scattered throughout Thailand. *Wats* are of great religious significance to the Thai people, and many *wats* are included in tours of Thailand.

When you visit a *wat,* there is an assault on the senses, as you find yourself in a space that is full of statues, religious images, and ornate architectural forms. Some Buddhas are covered with gold foil, which Thais put on the Buddhas to gain merit. The ambience is much different from the one you feel in large cathedrals, where there may also be many statues and images. However, these cathedrals have a rather somber quality about them, focusing, as they do, on Christ's death on the cross. *Wats* are also different from the very simple Protestant churches one finds in small towns in New England. *Wats* are polar op-

A beautiful *wat* in Thailand

posites of the Quaker churches with their incredible simplicity. In *wats* the atmosphere is almost festive, and you get a sense that there is a lot of activity not only in the *ubosoth,* but also in the entire compound, which houses monks and hundreds of stray dogs and other animals that the monks take in to care for.

Sacred Space and Profane Space

The human mind makes sense of things by setting up binary oppositions. Thus thin does not mean anything unless there is fat, and the same holds for wealthy and poor and all our other concepts. It was Saussure who pointed this out in his book *A Course in General Linguistics. Wats,* and all other religious edifices, occupy sacred space— space that differs from and is the opposite of profane space, the space in which we lead our everyday lives and conduct our business.

Emile Durkheim, in his classic study *The Elementary Forms of Religious Life,* explains the importance of this opposition. He writes:

> All known religious beliefs, whether simple or complex, present one common characteristic: they presuppose a classification of all the things, real and ideal, of which men think, into two classes or opposed groups, generally designated by two distinct terms which are translated well enough by the words *profane* and *sacred.* This division of the world into two domains, the one containing all that is sacred, the other all that is profane, is the distinctive trait of religious thought; the beliefs, myths, dogmas and legends are either representations or systems of representations which express the nature of sacred things, the virtues and powers which are attributed to them, or their relations with each other and profane things. (1965: 52)

Thus only those who are members of sacred communities can recite certain prayers, make certain movements, do certain activities, and use sacred objects. What makes objects sacred are determined by the members of each religion. Durkheim points out that Buddhism, which has no gods, is still a religion in that "it admits the existence of sacred things, namely the four noble truths and the practices derived from them" (1965: 52).

The sacred world and the profane world, Durkheim argues, are mutually antagonistic and exclude one another, to the extent they can. That is why monks cannot be touched by women and why Buddhism has developed an ascetic identity—to keep monks away, as much as possible, from the temptations of profane life. Asceticism, he argues, is an essential element of religious life and all religions have it, to varying degrees, in the sense that all religions have interdictions in them, whether it is about food or other aspects of life.

So *wats* can be looked upon as oases of the sacred in a generally profane Thai society. There are 30,000 *wats* in Thailand, on the sacred side, and 850,000 prostitutes (though I have seen estimates in the millions) on the profane side, existing side by side but keeping their distance (but not always). We can see the differences between the sacred and the profane in Table 6.3.

The meaning of most of these concepts are self-evident, but something should be said about Durkheim's ideas about churches. Durkheim defines a church as follows:

> The individuals who compose it feel themselves united to each other by the simple fact that they have a common faith. A society whose members are united by the fact that they think in the same way in regard to the sacred world, and by the fact that they translate these common ideas into common practices, is what is called a Church. In all history, we do not find a single religion without a Church . . . wherever we observe the religious life, we find that it has a definite group as its foundation. (1965: 59)

TABLE 6.3. The sacred and the profane.

Sacred	Profane
Soul	Body
Church	Society
Monks	Laypeople
Church	Organizations
Ritual	Activities
Sacred time (circular)	Ordinary time (linear)
Asceticism	Hedonism

Source: Berger (2004).

It would seem that the *wat* is the physical manifestation of the Buddhist Church, in Durkheim's sense of things. And it is to *wats,* sacred spaces, and images of what paradise might be like in the Thai imagination, that Thais repair when they seek spiritual guidance or solace or wish to celebrate life-cycle events such as marriages and births.

The Two Skylines of Thailand

There are two skylines in Thailand. One is the Thailand of the twentieth century, the profane skyline, which is filled with high-rise office buildings, malls, and other buildings that look like buildings in most cities. The other, however, is the sacred skyline, the skyline of the Thai temples and towers, of *wats* and stupas, which is a rather fantastic—to the American observer—skyline that symbolizes that which is exotic about Thailand.

In the guidebooks and booklets published by the Tourist Authority of Thailand, you often see the modern urban skylines in one photo and the traditional Thai temple architecture in another. It is part of the otherness of Thai culture, and to tourists coming from America, where many of the major buildings are modernist or even postmodern, the vernacular Thai buildings are quite striking.

There is what might be described as a "hyper-phallic" dimension to many of the Thai temples, many of which feature tall stupas and other towers. From a psychoanalytic perspective, it might be that these towers are phallic in nature and represent a kind of sublimation of the sexual energy of Buddhist monks, who take vows of celibacy, into architecture. We see the same thing in profane architecture, at the opposite extreme, in places such as Las Vegas. Lee Klay, who was part of the Federal Sign and Signal Company in Las Vegas, recounted, in *The New York Times,* that the owners of the Dunes hotel in Las Vegas told him about the sign they wanted. "We want a big phallic symbol going up in the sky as far as you can make it," they told him, and that is what he gave them (Brown, 1993).

It is not unreasonable, then, to see huge signs and tall towers as being phallic symbols, even though the people who commissioned them and the architects who designed them did not think of them as such. At either end of the spectrum—at the sacred end of the Buddhist monks of

Thailand in their *(wats)* monasteries and at the profane end of the signs and buildings in Las Vegas, we find phallic imagery.

Wats play an important role in the lives of the Thai people, 95 percent of whom are Buddhists, but also in the experiences of tourists to Thailand, who gain from these *wats* an insight into Buddhism and sense of what earlier Thai cultures were like. Thailand offers tourists both extremes of the sacred and profane continuum: *Wats* full of ascetic monks and cities full of bar girls and prostitutes.

THE THAI WAI

The *wai* is a common form of greeting and mutual recognition that Thais use. It involves pressing the palms together and touching the body generally around the chest, but up to the face, for people of high status. When you are in Thailand you notice many people giving *wais* to one another—when they meet and when they leave one another, when they receive gifts from one another, and so on.

The Thai *wai*

The Complexities Involved in the **Wai**

All *wai*s are not the same. For example, Thais who want to indicate respect to another person of higher status touch their hands higher, near their faces. Thus, the higher the *wai,* the more respect is given. The person being *waid* generally reciprocates, but not always. Monks, for example, who are at the top of the social hierarchy in Thailand, do not return *wais* from laypeople—even from the king.

In some cases, where the person being greeted has very high status, it is customary to bend one's head or bow. The *wai* can be seen as a signifier of the hierarchical nature of Buddhist society and the complicated system of determining what is the proper kind of *wai* to give people. Children must be indoctrinated into the intricacies of using the *wai,* which means they also are taught about the status system in Thailand. They must learn who should be respected and how much respect is due them. That is, they must be taught the codes that determine how the *wai* should be done in various circumstances.

In *Culture Shock: Succeed in Business Thailand,* the authors deal with this matter:

> The *wai* has a lot to do with status and hierarchy. For example, when Thais meet, a person who is junior in age or social rank will always *wai* first. The senior usually *wai*s in return by raising the hands only to chest level or merely nodding his head and smiling to acknowledge the greeting. The greater the difference in hierarchy between two people, the less likely the superior will return the *wai*. At the top of the social hierarchy, Buddhist monks never return a *wai* from anyone, not even royalty. In turn, the royal family never *wai*s members of the public. (1998: 210)

Thus, a *wai* is a greeting and an acknowledgment to other people that they are recognized, but it is much more than that, since it recognizes and reinforces status hierarchies and power relationships in Thai society. You learn not to return *wais* from people who are lower than you in the Thai social hierarchy and to always *wai* people who are higher than you, who will respond to your *wai* with a nod of the head or a smile.

The Japanese Bow

The *wai* is different in form from the Japanese bow. When the Japanese bow, they keep their arms by their sides, but, like the *wai,* the degree to which they bow is connected to hierarchy and status. In his book, *Empire of Signs,* Roland Barthes deals with Japanese culture and discusses bowing in Japan. He contrasts Japanese courtesy with occidental impoliteness, which suggests that "to be impolite is to be true" (1982: 63) and that bowing and other forms of courtesy are tainted by hypocrisy. He describes Japanese (and by implication Thai) bowing as follows:

> The other politeness, by the scrupulosity of its codes, the distinct graphism of its gestures, and even when it seems to us exaggeratedly respectful (i.e., to our eyes "humiliating") because we read it, in our manner, according to a metaphysics of the person—this politeness is a certain exercise of the void (as we might expect with a strong code but one signifying "nothing"). Two bodies bow very low before one another (arms, knees, head always remaining in a decreed place), according to subtly coded degrees of depth. Or again (on an old image): in order to give a present, I bow down, virtually to the level of the floor, and to answer me, my partner does the same . . . (1982: 65)

Barthes speculates that, in Japan, religion has become politeness or that religion has actually been replaced by politeness. For Barthes it would seem that in Japan the bow has lost any meaning and is an empty form.

The Irony of the **Wai**

The Thais are described as happy-go-lucky, fun-loving people, and these descriptions seem to be accurate. But at the same time, they find themselves living in a rigidly hierarchical society, where they have to learn complex codes that teach them the proper ways to *wai* others (and also what forms of language to use) depending on their status and power. Thus, often during the course of their interactions with others, they are reminded of their place in the scheme of things, their rung on the hierarchy.

It also is a means of avoiding touching one another, a means of keeping one's distance, and may reflect a diffuse kind of alienation pervading Thai society. There is a marked difference between the ritualized and highly formalistic nature of the *wai* and the incredible amount of body contact taking places in bars and brothels. Like so many aspects of Thai life, there seems to be a compartmentalization or dissociation between opposing elements of life in Thailand. Thailand is a country where people don't touch one another when they meet during the day (unlike Americans, who shake hands all the time and are always giving one another air kisses) but is a country in which extramarital affairs are accepted and is also a country that functions as a "sex magnet" to the world.

THAI FOOD

In recent years, Thai restaurants have become very popular in the United States—because this food offers new taste sensations to Americans, ones that they had not experienced before.

There are many Thais who have immigrated to the United States and, like many such groups, have started restaurants.

A simple restaurant with Thai delicacies

Oppositions in Thai Food

It is a distinctive cuisine with complex and very rich flavors, including combinations of seemingly opposite flavors and textures that are surprising to the American and Western palate (see Table 6.4).

Thais use garlic, chili peppers, lemon grass, lemon juice, lime juice, coriander, tamarind juice, coconut milk, shrimp paste, and fish sauce *(nampla)* to generate their food's rich flavors—and Thai food varies in hotness from rather mild to exceedingly, mouth-blisteringly hot. There are a number of important regional cuisines in Thailand, as might be expected: in some areas the Chinese and Laotian influence is very strong and in other areas, such as the south, the Malay influence is great. Thai cuisine is, then, a very sophisticated and complex one; its beautiful presentation and unusual flavors make it very popular with tourists from foreign countries.

Most Popular Thai Dishes

In 1999, a Thai cultural commission conducted a survey to find out which Thai dishes were most popular with foreign tourists. The list that follows shows which dishes were most popular, in order of popularity.

1. *tom yam kung* (spicy shrimp soup) 99 percent
2. *kaeng khiao wan kai* (green chicken curry) 85 percent
3. *phat tha* (fried noodles Thai style) 70 percent
4. *phat kaphrao* (meat fried with sweet basil) 52 percent
5. *kaeng phet pet yang* (roast duck curry) 50 percent
6. *tom kah kai* (chicken and coconut soup) 47 percent
7. *yam nua* (spicy beef salad) 45 percent
8. *mu or kai sa-te* (roast pork or chicken coated with turmeric) 43 percent
9. *kai phat met mamauang himmaphan* (chicken with cashew nuts) 42 percent
10. *phananeng nua* (meat in coconut sauce) 39 percent (http://www.dininginthailand.com/foodfacts.asp)

This list also serves the purpose of giving us an idea of some of the different kinds of Thai dishes that are available.

TABLE 6.4. Dry and wet food.

Dry	Wet
Sour (Salty)	Sweet
Mild	Hot
Soft	Crisp

Source: Author's compilation.

The "classic" American dinner of salad, broiled beefsteak, baked potatoes, green beans (or some other green vegetable), and apple pie and ice cream, is much different from Thai food in that it has no sauces (except, in some cases, bottled ketchup) and uses no spices, aside from garlic and some spices in the salad dressing.

"Wok You See Is What You Get"

In a 2004 article in the *Financial Times,* restaurant critic Nicholas Lander describes Thais as very discriminating eaters and says that they do not care about restaurant decor. What is most important to them is the quality of the food in the restaurant and so they frequent restaurants known to be good for various specialties, depending on the particular dish they might crave. He mentions a discussion he had with Christophe Mengel, executive chef of the Ritz Carlton in Singapore, who suggests that cooks in Asia use "blazingly hot" woks in comparison to cooks in the West whose woks are not as hot, and that accounts for a major difference between the way foods are cooked.

Lander describes a visit to the Aw Taw Kaw food market with Bob Halliday, who wrote a food column for the *Bangkok Post* under the pseudonym Ung Aang Talal (Sea Toad) for many years. They saw a food stall where a man was preparing a dish:

> Here, in a large wok, a man was creating delicious sweetmeats: bananas coated in sesame and then fried in coconut milk; peanut crackers; and small rice flour rounds filled with coconut cream, palm sugar, diced onions and chives.

These combinations are most unusual and help explain why Thai food tastes so different and offers remarkable taste sensations for Westerners, especially Americans.

THAI PROSTITUTES AND THE SEX INDUSTRY

There are wildly varying estimates about the number of prostitutes found in Thailand—from 800,000 to 3 million. In either case, we can see that prostitution is an enormous industry and problem and still plays a major role in Thai everyday life and in tourism to Thailand. There are, then, twice as many prostitutes in Thailand as Buddhist monks if the 800,000 figure is accurate. And many, many times that figure—almost ten times as many—if the 3 million figure is correct. (It is estimated that around one-third of the prostitutes in Thailand are under eighteen, which means that, in many cases, very young girls are working as prostitutes.) This explains why others might see Thailand, in general, as an erotic country, though I would add to this formulation a suggestion, supported by many tourists and travel writers, that it is also an exotic country. Thailand also exports many prostitutes to countries like Japan; so prostitution in Thailand has an international or global cast to it.

Thai prostitutes are seen as different from sex workers in the West. As Jeremy Seabrook explains in his book *Travels in the Skin Trade: Tourism and the Sex Industry:*

> One thing that clearly draws Western men to Thai women is the perceived capacity of the women for what I can only describe as tenderness, a quality conspicuously absent from the sex industry in the West. Men feel particularly cherished by what they experience as the compliance, eagerness and considerateness of Thai women. (2001: 3)

These qualities draw others to Thailand for sex when it is readily available from prostitutes in Western countries, and these qualities are tied to Thai culture and its emphasis on pleasing others. According to a Thai informant of mine, Thai women are taught to be dominant in bed and to determine how the sex act is to be conducted. The same applies to social interactions, where women lead the way—in part as a means of taking the burden off their husbands and thus helping them save "face." Thai women also run their households—controlling finances, determining how children are to be raised, and, at one time, finding "minor" wives for their husbands. This is no longer the case and modern Thai women discourage their husbands from taking on "minor" wives.

We also have to recognize that there are economic forces at work behind the Thai sex industry. A considerable percentage of Thai women work in the sex industry because, lacking other skills, they know of no other way to earn money for their families.

The Erotic and the Exotic in Thailand

In my primer on semiotics, I discussed Saussure's work on concepts and his suggestion that concepts have no meaning in themselves; they derive their meaning, in essence, by being the opposite of some other concept. As he put it, "In language there are only differences." Given this insight, it is possible to see Thai culture in terms of two sets of complimentary polar opposition, the erotic and the exotic.

Sociologist Erik Cohen, one of the most outstanding scholars of Thai tourism, discusses these two concepts in his book *Thai Tourism: Hill Tribes, Island, and Open-Ended Prostitution*—a collection of his essays on various aspects of tourism in Thailand written over a period of almost twenty years. As he explains:

> In the past, the image of Thailand in the eyes of Western visitors was that of an exotic, enchanted kingdom in the Orient. The arrival of American servicemen on R&R visits, compounded by the stationing of about 40,000 US military personnel in bases in Thailand, shifted the emphasis in the tourist sector from sight-seeing of cultural attractions, reflecting the earlier image, to more mundane pursuits, primarily sex and recreational activities. . . . The GI period added a new dimension to Thai tourism: tourist-oriented prostitution. During that period, Thailand acquired the still fairly widespread dual image of "Temples and Brothels," an image expressing two contrasting basic themes, which made travel to Thailand so attractive in the post-Vietnam War period: the exotic and the erotic. While there surely exists some affinity between these themes—for example, the alluring exoticism of Thai women—they represent structural opposites, the face and the obverse of Thailand's tourist attractiveness. They are also concrete reflections of the pervasive dualism of

Thai society (cf. Cohen, 1991), in which Buddhist abnegation and mundane enjoyment *(sanuk)* coexist as opposite, but mutually complementing cultural poles. (1962: 2)

Cohen adds that the tourism authorities in Thailand used a slogan "Thailand—The Most Exotic Country in Asia" and published travel literature full of images of temples, hill people, and classical Thai dancers to give potential tourists an idea of what they would be seeing when visiting Thailand. I should point out that I concluded that Thailand was this fascinating combination of the erotic and the exotic before I had read Cohen's superb book.

As I see things, it is the Thai prostitute that can be seen as the exemplar of the erotic. The terms, in Greek *erotikos,* comes from the Greek god Eros, the god of love, and is connected to powerful feelings of sexual desire. Her opposite is the Thai monk, who, I would suggest, serves as an example of the exotic. The term exotic comes from the Greek *exotikos,* which means "outside." Dictionaries define the exotic as very unusual or foreign. The *wat* or monastery, where the monk lives, is very unusual to the Western person in terms of its architecture and ambience. The bordello where the prostitute works, on the other hand, is a site of eroticism (though not all Thai prostitutes work in bordellos by any means—many work in hotels and apartments).

The Sacred and the Profane in Thailand

The scholar of religion, Mircea Eliade, in his book *The Sacred and the Profane,* and the great French sociologist Emile Durkheim, in his book *The Elementary Forms of Religious Life,* suggested that one of the fundamental oppositions in the human mind is between two poles—the sacred and the profane. Each of these realms has its attitudes toward space and time and various rules and codes that are to be followed. The sacred, in Thailand, is the realm of the monk and the profane is the realm of the prostitute. They are at either end of the sacred–profane continuum, with most Thais in the middle—not able to follow all the numerous strictures of Buddhism as far as the sacred is concerned, and not selling their bodies as far as the profane is concerned.

The Thai monk wears a saffron robe and walks barefooted. He has taken a vow of sexual abstinence. The Thai prostitute wears various costumes, signifying her status to others, and is at the opposite end of the sexual spectrum, engaging in sex as an occupation.

We can see these oppositions more clearly in Table 6.5. The oppositions may be a bit extreme here and there, but I think it is generally accurate.

These complimentary polar oppositions give tourists a sense of what Thai life and culture is, at the extremes, so to speak. Not all buildings in Thailand are *wats* and only a small proportion of Thai women work as prostitutes. But like so many things in life, it is the extreme examples that color our perspectives on the countries we visit.

THAILAND AND AMERICA: A STUDY IN OTHERNESS

When we are tourists in foreign countries, the otherness we experience reflects back on us, like a mirror, and enables us to see our own selves with more clarity and in higher definition. One of the delicious ironies of foreign travel is that the more we learn about other societies and cultures, the more we discover about our own societies and cultures. Some cultures, because they are so different, do a better job of teaching us about ourselves as we learn more and more about them, and Thailand is one of those countries where the culture shock tears away the shrouds that we use to hide ourselves from ourselves. So,

TABLE 6.5. The erotic and the exotic.

Erotic	Exotic
Profane	Sacred
Prostitute	Monk
Bordello	Wat (monastery)
Costume	Saffron robe
Female	Male
Sex	Salvation
800,000	300,000 to 400,000

Source: Author's compilation.

when Americans visit Thailand, it becomes a much more profound experience than they might possibly have anticipated.

We can continue with our focus on bipolar oppositions as a way of finding meaning in life and compare and contrast the United States and Thailand—two countries that are polar opposites in many respects. I have suggested that for Americans (and, by extension, for people in many other countries of the West), Thailand is a paradigm of otherness. And that is because, on so many different fronts, it is radically different from our beliefs, our values, and the ways we live our everyday lives.

A Comparison of Two Countries and Cultures

It is these differences that lead me to describe Thailand as exotic, as outside our normal way of looking at the world, and it is this identity of Thailand as exotic that is the source of much of its appeal. Table 6.6, by comparing the United States and Thailand in a number of different ways, offers insights into both countries, as one, so to speak, shines a light on the other.

What the Oppositions Reveal

Americans (and I will use this term instead of the awkward construction "inhabitants of the United States") are, we must realize, very religious. Compared to Europe and many other Western countries, a much higher percentage of Americans say that they believe that God exists and they attend church. A considerable number of American Christians have had religious experiences and describe themselves as "born again," including President George W. Bush. And religion in America is intimately involved in politics—with evangelical Christian groups supporting the Republican Party and conservative political causes.

In Thailand, on the other hand, Buddhism is not intimately or as overtly involved in politics and the Thais, followers of Buddhism, do not have gods. The Buddha is not seen as a god but as an elevated teacher and exemplar. Buddhism focuses on individuals finding the means of their own salvation and not, at least overtly, to the extent that American Christianity does, on things such as social programs.

TABLE 6.6. Comparison of Thailand and the United States.

United States	Thailand
Christianity	Buddhism
God believed in	No gods
Was a colony of Britain	Always independent
Large country	Small country
President	King
Express emotions	Hide emotions (Thai smile)
Egalitarian	Hierarchical
Authority invalid	Authority accepted
Achievement (American dream)	Pleasure
Serial monogamy	Sanctioned infidelity
Assertive	Accepting *(kieng jai)*
Nervous	Calm *(san ruan)* outwardly
Hidden anxiety	Hidden tension and rage
Last names used	First names used
Orderly politics	Chaotic politics
The Eagle as symbol	The Elephant as symbol
Violence due to sexual repression	Violence due to repressed hostility
Shake hands (touch)	*Wai* (don't touch)
Religions political	Religion apolitical
Social conscience	Salvation–an individual matter

Source: Author's compilation.

The Thai government has this responsibility, not the religious establishment in Thailand.

Thailand is a royal country, with a king, and is very hierarchical. Thai children are taught who deserves how much respect in Thailand, with monks being at the top of the pyramid, followed by the king, the military, businessmen, and so on, down to the farmers and peasants, at the bottom of the ladder. These status differences are reflected in the way Thais use language and *wai* one another.

This is quite different from America, where the values are egalitarian and there are no official hierarchies. Americans are equal under the law, but there are, of course, very great differences in the social classes (and these differences are getting greater with every year), which means that the children of wealthy parents have greater "life chances" than those at the bottom of the ladder. Americans believe in the "American dream," which suggests that anyone born in America, or who moves to America, can ultimately be a success, because we do not have (official) classes as barriers to that success. In recent years, as poverty has grown in America and the middle classes find themselves pressured, belief in the American Dream is wavering.

As an egalitarian people, Americans do not like authority and tend not to accept it as valid. This is quite different from the situation in Thailand, where the king's authority is not questioned and where authority's validity is connected to the hierarchical nature of Thai society. Because Americans are egalitarian, they must achieve to demonstrate their goodness and power to others, which explains why Americans are so obsessed with shopping and acquiring material goods and allegedly life-transforming, life-enhancing experiences— such as traveling to Thailand. Americans tend to be anxiety-ridden about their place in society and the way that others will think about them.

Americans tend to be friendly, at least on a superficial basis, and to demonstrate their emotions openly, by their facial expressions and body language. Thais, on the other hand, are much more reserved, covering their emotions with "the Thai smile." Americans shake hands and touch one another; Thais *wai* one another and do not touch. This custom leads, I would suggest, to a kind of distancing from others and ultimately to a kind of alienation from the self and from others. Not being able to express emotions can often lead to powerful but repressed feelings of hostility and rage. In recent years, the term "rage" has become popular in America, and is used to describe feelings of powerlessness and then anger that Americans feel when they are driving their cars and are bothered by other drivers, for one reason or another (road rage). There are various other rages now afflicting Americans.

This susceptibility to rages and the anxiety that permeates much of American society is quite different, then, from the ambiance of Thai culture, where there is a focus on being accepting and not making people feel uncomfortable—what the Thais describe as *kieng jai.* Thais are often described as easygoing, "happy-go-lucky" people and Thai culture is one that believes that pleasure and happiness are very important.

It may be that the hierarchical nature of Thai society facilitates these attitudes, for unlike Americans, who are always anxious about their status, Thais know exactly where they belong and need not worry about such things. This has two sides to it: on one side, people are stuck in whatever rung of the hierarchical ladder they find themselves, but on the other side, they are liberated from continually feeling anxious about themselves and their social status and feeling the need to prove themselves to others.

There is some question now about the communitarian sensibility of Americans, who now "bowl alone" as one sociologist put it, suggesting that social networks and a sense of social obligation in America are waning. There is also a question about the degree to which the Thai sense that salvation is an individual responsibility has been affected by the need for social institutions to be developed to look after the public welfare. Thus, there is a difference between dominant values that can be ascribed to a country and the way people in that country actually live and the institutions that they develop to take care of their needs.

Desperate Housewives and the Pressures of the Modern World

The Thais face the problem of an estimated 3,000 Thai prostitutes having AIDS. If something is not done to control this matter, they can and will infect many other Thais who use their services, as well as sex tourists and sexpatriates. Thus, in Thailand there is reason to believe that the threat of AIDS being transmitted by prostitutes has led to many "desperate" housewives; in America the housewives are desperate for other reasons, connected, also, to sex.

The Thais also face the need to deal with a restive Muslim population in the southern part of the country. So although one's national culture may be informed in profound ways by Buddhism, the reality is that Thailand must have a police force, and possibly a military, to deal with Muslim insurgents. So the modern world forces countries into certain modes of development, regardless of what the official religion might dictate.

This little exercise, comparing Thai and American culture, suggests some of the reasons why Thailand is so appealing to Americans (and others who approximate the American lifestyle). And this is because Thailand is such a study in radical "otherness" that it intoxicates foreign tourists while enabling them to understand themselves and their country in a more complete manner.

PART III:
THAILAND ON MY MIND

One of the most ancient motives for travel, when men had any choice about it, was to see the unfamiliar. Man's incurable desire to go somewhere else is a testimony to his optimism and insatiable curiosity. We always expect things to be different there. "Traveling," Descartes wrote in the early seventeenth century, "is almost like conversing men of other centuries." Men who move because they are starved or frightened or oppressed expect to be safer, better fed, and more free in the new place. Men who live in a secure, rich, and decent society travel to escape boredom, to elude the familiar, and to discover the exotic.

They have often succeeded. Great stirrings of the mind have frequently followed great ages of travel. Throughout history by going to far places and seeing strange sights men have prodded their imagination. They have found amazement and delight and have reflected that life back home need not always remain as it has been. They have learned that there is more than one way to skin a cat, that there are more things in heaven and earth than was dreamt of in their philosophy, that the possibilities of life are not exhausted on Main Street.

Boorstin, *The Image: A Guide to Pseudo-Events
in America,* 1975: 78

Self-contempt and a sense of fraudulence distinguish the attitude of contemporary self-conscious travelers. There is a touching desperation in the attempts of professional tourists, well-funded anthropologists, and recording travelers, to distinguish themselves from the traveling masses and run-of-the-mill adventurers. The most characteristic mark of the tourist is the wish to avoid tourists and places they congregate. But this is merely evidence of the fact that travel is no longer a means of achieving distinction. It is a way of achieving and realizing a norm, the common identity we all share—the identity of the stranger.

Leed, *The Mind of the Traveler: From Gilgamesh
to Global Tourism,* 1991: 286-287

Chapter 7

Notes from My Thailand Journal

Like many tourists, I keep a journal when I go on my travels, and what follows comes from the notes I took in my journal—edited to eliminate redundancies and information of little significance as far as my travels in Thailand and the matter of tourism are concerned. As a matter of fact, I have kept journals since 1954 and this book, *Thailand Tourism,* was thought out and planned, and in some cases written, in my journal—Volume 80, whose title is "High-Value Target." That title is ironic in that I was mocking the various news reports about high-value targets in recent times, but it turns out that being a tourist in some countries—not Thailand (or at least not the northern sections of Thailand)—actually makes tourists high-value targets.

I will not be offering a chronology of our tour and will not be listing all the hotels we stayed at and the restaurants where we dined, but I will mention some from time to time. Like any tourist's remembrances of a trip, I will skip around from topic to topic.

ARRIVAL IN BANGKOK

When we arrived in Bangkok it was around 10:00 p.m. The trip to Bangkok from San Francisco had seemed endless. We had booked a flight on Korean Airlines, so we had to fly to Seoul first and deplaned at Kimpo Airport. Then we had to wait around for our flight to Bangkok. Even though we left from San Francisco, it took a long time to get to Bangkok, in the vicinity of twenty hours, counting the wait be-

Thailand Tourism
© 2007 by The Haworth Press, Inc. All rights reserved.
doi:10.1300/5789_07

fore we left San Francisco and the break between flights in Korea. There were seventeen hours of flying time. Travel to distant locations is exhausting, even under the best of circumstances.

We had traveled with Korean Airlines a few years before this trip, and when it was time to serve meals, the stewardesses changed into native costumes and the steward put on a tuxedo. Not this time. After what seemed like an eternity we arrived in Bangkok. We were traveling light; so we did not have to wait at the carousels for any baggage. We hopped on a cab to our hotel, the Viengtai, after we went through immigration and customs. I noticed that there was not much traffic and not too many people walking around. After we checked into the hotel we were hungry. So we walked down the street where the hotel was located and found The Easy Guest House, which had a small restaurant. We had soup, chicken curry, shrimp, and vegetables, and something to drink. Perhaps it was because we were famished, but the food was marvelous. We were to eat there several times.

The next day we went to the National Palace, took a boat ride on the river, and wandered around the area near our hotel. Bangkok by day was much different from Bangkok by night. The sidewalks were crowded with people selling things and cooking things. Some of the food looked good but we were afraid to try street food since we both had friends who had picked up terrible parasites in their travels in Southeast Asia. Why tempt the fates when restaurants were so inexpensive?

Unlike the night before, the traffic in Bangkok was chaotic and my eyes were smarting from the terrible smog. I decided that after we saw some of the more important tourist sites in Bangkok, it would be prudent to leave at the earliest possible opportunity. The next day we visited a museum and looked around a huge shopping center. After dinner, we went to the railroad station, bought second-class rail passes good for two weeks—they cost $80 for each of us—and after waiting around the station for a couple of hours, set off to Chiang Mai. Tourists who are traveling on their own often find themselves waiting around in railroad stations, bus stations, and airports. And those who are on packaged tours often find themselves waiting for others on the tour who are not prompt about getting on the bus.

CULTURAL CLASH

In my journal I speculated about culture clash in Thailand and wrote the following:

Cultural Clash in Thailand?? Clash? Integration?

1. Has American/European culture (pop culture) had a major impact in Thailand? Or is it superficial? A veneer?
2. Have other cultures had an impact of any significance? If so, which ones?
3. Is there a difference between Bangkok and other cities in Thailand? Tourist cities and other (nontourist) ones?
4. What American popular culture is popular in Thailand? What American popular culture isn't popular?
5. What is the "image" of America/Americans in the Thai media? Is there interest in America/Americans in the Thai media? Is there interest in American culture? American elite culture?

So long before I had thought of writing about tourism or tourism in Thailand, I had started formulating questions that I thought would be interesting to investigate.

I had arranged to give some lectures on American popular culture and media studies at Chulalongkorn University at the end of our stay in Thailand. So those questions naturally came to mind. I called the dean there, a lovely woman named Darunee Hiranruk, and let her know that we had arrived safely and would be arriving at her university in several weeks—after our tour of Thailand. I recall her office very distinctly. It was a large, sunny room full of beautiful plants. It looked more like a greenhouse than an office. When we went to lunch I noticed that her colleagues, from her department, were also women. I wondered what percentage of university professors were women.

CHIANG MAI ADVENTURES

Chiang Mai, I concluded, was essentially a smaller version of Bangkok. The noise from the automobiles, trucks, buses, and motorbikes was overwhelming and Chiang Mai also had polluted air. There were lots of *wats* to see in Chiang Mai and, to my surprise, there was an American ice cream shop on one of the main streets. We visited a number of *wats* in Chiang Mai and then took a tour to Doi Pui, a hill tribes village. A large sign at the entrance to the village read "Welcome to Doi Pui." It had large Pepsi-Cola ads on either end of the sign. I found that amusing, perhaps because it seemed too incongruous. We also went to the Royal Winter Palace and a famous temple, Wat Doi Suthep, which is on almost every tourist itinerary.

This temple has a huge torso of the Buddha and all kinds of other statues, of varying sizes. There is a distinctive aesthetic to the temple areas of *wats*—one that varies considerably from what you find in the giant Catholic cathedrals. These cathedrals have, I have always thought, a tomblike quality, due, in part, to the fact that light is suppressed and one feels overwhelmed by the huge columns and the enormous size of the buildings. The sense of the sacred permeates them. You see candles burning, huge statues of Christ on the Cross in a central area, and a kind of hushed reverence that is all-pervasive. In addition, these cathedrals generally have other works of art, other statues of Christ and various saints, and other religious figures. And many have very beautiful stained-glass windows.

Wats, such as Doi Suthep, have a different version of the religious space, and visitors to *wats* cannot help but sense a very powerful aura of the sacred in them. There are the statues of the Buddha, often gigantic in size, that gaze upon you. The eyes are done in a highly stylized manner and the expressions on the face of most Buddhas is hard to fathom. There are other statues and murals and other artifacts, all rather cluttered to the point of being overwhelming to the Western sensibility. The Buddha is not a god, but the way Buddhists pray to him and relate to him suggests that they think of him as such, even though officially he is only considered to be the supremely enlightened human being. For tourists from the West, the various Buddhist practices—the chanting, the sounding of gongs, the ringing of bells—all of these are quite strange.

THE PLEASURE OF CHANCE ENCOUNTERS

When you are a tourist, you often have remarkable experiences. This is one of the most appealing aspects of tourism—you escape from everyday routine and submit yourself to the unexpected, to chance events, to remarkable coincidences. On the train from Song-kla to Surit Thani, my wife and I decided to go to the dining car. There were only two empty seats at a table. I asked the person who was sitting at the table whether he'd mind if my wife and I sat down at his table. He said that would be fine.

We started chatting. He asked me where I was from. I said I was from Mill Valley. At that, he laughed. "I'm from Sebastapol," he said—a town about thirty miles up the highway from Mill Valley. Two English girls happened to be sitting at the table opposite ours. "Excuse me," one of them said, "But I happened to overhear you say you were from Mill Valley. May I ask where in Mill Valley you live?" I told her what street we lived on and she smiled. It turned out that her cousin lived five houses away from us. It is chance encounters of this nature that makes travel such an interesting and exciting thing to do.

NOTES ON SIGNS AND SYMBOLS OF THAILAND

In my notebook I have a chart listing "Topics, Images, Things to Think About" that functions, it turns out, as a precursor to some of the subjects I wrote about in this book. The list reads as follows:

1. Hyper-Motorcycle-ization
2. Television addiction of Thais
3. Monks
4. *Wats*
5. Mental shocks
6. Pollution in Bangkok and Chiang Mai
7. Second-class sleepers
8. Night Markets
9. *Tuk-tuks*
10. English-language newspapers
11. Bus station in Bangkok
12. Food cooking over coals in sidewalk food stalls
13. Food vendors at railroad stations
14. Songaklews
15. Tropical landscape

So, well before I had ever entertained the idea of writing a book on tourism in Thailand, a number of signs and symbols of Thailand had struck my attention.

ON THE NIGHT FERRY TO KO SAMUI

On the night ferry from Surit Thani to Ko Samui, my wife and I purchased places to sleep (thin mattresses) on the upper deck. There was a very friendly young Thai woman on the trip who came around with a three-ringed binder that had photographs of a resort she worked for. One could rent a small villa, with a fan, for 4 dollars a night. She told us that she works at the hotel during the day as a chamber maid and at night she takes ferries and spends her evenings trying to convince passengers to spend time at her hotel. We decided we wanted an air-conditioned room; so when we finally arrived in Ko Samui, we piled on to the back of a pickup truck (with benches to sit on) and she came with us and had the truck stop in front of a very lovely hotel on Lamai Beach, The Golden Sand Beach Resort. It was just 100 feet or so from the beach—a gorgeous expanse of sand and palm trees, which is what you imagine when you think of visiting Ko Samui.

SPECULATIONS ON TYPICAL TOURISTIC ACTIVITIES

On the ferry to Ko Samui, I wrote some notes in which I speculated about how tourists, who are not on organized tours, spend their time

The Tourist Does Many Things

1. Sees things ("sights")
2. Buys things (souvenirs, gifts, bargains)
3. Waits—for trains, buses, ferries, airplanes
4. Takes photographs of sights
5. Finds hotels and restaurants
6. Cashes travelers' checks, uses credit cards
7. Consults timetables, guidebooks
8. Plans what to see and when to see it
9. Deals with emergencies and snafus: fully booked trains, etc.

10. Seeks pleasures
11. Sends postcards

That, in a highly reductionist formulation, describes the experience of being a tourist. Being a tourist involves all kinds of decisions about where to go, when to go there, and how to get there, and then where to stay and where to eat when you get to your destination. Even on package tours, travelers often have to decide where to eat—since, generally speaking, only some of their meals are covered by their tour.

We arrived in Bangkok two hours late, because of a problem with the train system. We had come to Bangkok after traveling for two weeks in the southern part of Thailand (and in Kota Baru, Malaysia, for a couple of days). We had a suite waiting for us in the SASA building but I discovered that nobody knew where the SASA building was at Chulalongkorn University. Our *tuk-tuk* driver stopped any number of times and asked people. He finally dropped us off in a place that he thought was near it, which happened to be the case. So, just in the nick of time, we were able to get our suite there (SASA has rooms for people visiting Chulalongkorn University) and get ready for my first lecture. When you travel, you can never be sure that any plane will leave on time or that any train or bus will arrive on time.

EXOTIC CALIFORNIA:
HIGH SCHOOL SUBCULTURES IN CALIFORNIA

I gave three lectures at Chulalongkorn University, where one of my books, *Media Analysis Techniques,* was used. One was on ways of analyzing media, one was on writing for the media, and the third was on popular culture in America. In that lecture I explained to my students that our high schools have many subcultures, many of which are tied to our popular culture. American students do not wear official uniforms but do conform to the dress codes of their particular group or subculture. I listed some of the groups one finds in California high schools:

1. Cheerleaders
2. Jocks
3. Headbangers
4. Nerds/Geeks

   5. Dorks/Dweebs
   6. Punks
   7. Goths
   8. Hicks
   9. Preppies
 10. Skinheads
 11. Surfers
 12. Skaters
 13. Creeps
 14. *Vatos* (Latinos)
 15. Brothers (African Americans)
 16. Drammies
 17. Dreads (African Americans with dreadlocks)

I drew up this list with help from students in my popular culture courses at San Francisco State University. It represents a compendium of different groups found in a variety of high schools in California and, as extensive as it is, it is incomplete.

This list was quite shocking to my students at Chulalongkorn, who had been exposed to a great deal of American popular culture (it seemed that everyone was watching television in Thailand everywhere we went . . . it seemed impossible to escape from films and television shows) but who had no idea about the diversity of cultures found in our high schools, and by extension, in American society. You do not find such a large number of cliques or special-interest groups in high schools in Thailand or in many countries. For Thai students, these Californian subcultures would probably be fascinating, and Thais visiting certain parts of the United States and seeing in-line roller skaters (with their helmets and other aspects of their costume), skateboarders, surfers (with their hair dyed blonde), punks (with purple and orange hair), and Goths (dressed in black), would find America "exotic."

I can remember how innocent the Thai students at Chulalongkorn University seemed to me, as I participated in a good luck ceremony in which faculty members at the school (and I was invited to do so as a guest lecturer) sat on a platform and tied strings around the wrists of students who shuffled up to them on their knees. I would imagine our various high school subcultures would be as exotic to Thai students as the Thai hill tribes would be to American students. I was asked whether I would be interested in returning to Chulalongkorn University the next summer, for a month or so, but I found Bangkok so overwhelming, and the pollution so irritating, that I declined.

THE NIGHT MARKET AT HUA HIN

We had a fabulous dinner in the night market at Hua Hin: crab in curry sauce, grilled shrimp, and deep-fried squid. The restaurant set up chairs and tables on the street. The streets were full of such restaurants. It was warm and there was a certain amount of festivity in the air, as people wandered around, dined, bought things at stalls. Afterward, I found a barbershop and had a haircut. A number of Thais gathered around to see the haircut, since, I must assume, a red-headed person getting a haircut in one of their salons was something quite unusual for them. And probably for the woman who cut my hair, as well. Her children were there, looking on—with good seats.

Afterward, as we were looking around, a young man on a motorbike suddenly drove it right on to the sidewalk and raced by us, narrowly missing my wife.

"I think I've had enough of Southeast Asia," she said. And so we had—until we went to Vietnam and returned for more encounters with hyper-motorbike-ization and the many delights of Vietnam.

There was a time when travel confronted the traveller with civilizations radically different from his own. It was their strangeness, after all, which impressed him. But these opportunities have been getting rarer and rarer for a very long time. Be it in India or in America, the traveller of our day finds things more familiar than he will admit. The aims and itineraries which we devise for ourselves are, above all, ways of being free to choose at what date we shall penetrate a given society. Our mechanistic civilization is overcoming all others, but we can at least choose the speed at which it will be effecting its conquests. The search for the exotic will always bring us back to the same conclusion, but we can choose between an early or late stage of its development. The traveller becomes a kind of dealer in antiques—one who, haven given up his gallery of primitive art for lack of stock, falls back on fusty souvenirs brought back from the flea-markets of the inhabited world.

Lévi-Strauss, *Tristes Tropiques:*
An Anthropological Study
of Primitive Societies in Brazil, 1970: 90

He traveled.
He came to know the melancholy of the steamboats, the cold of dawn under the tents, the tedium of landscapes and ruins, the bitterness of interrupted friendships.
He returned.

Flaubert, *The Sentimental Education*

Chapter 8

A Journey of Ten Thousand Miles
Ends with a Step

Lévi-Strauss, the great anthropologist, laments that the world is becoming a monoculture in which differences between peoples all over the world are flattening and fading away and wherever you go, life is increasingly very much the same. But is he right?

THAILAND AS A MONOCULTURE

Things, he suggests, are getting more and more familiar, no matter where you go. And, on a superficial level, Lévi-Strauss's argument may be correct There may be American hamburger chains and Starbucks coffee houses spread throughout the world, but that doesn't mean that all cultures are losing their character, by any means. I do not think you could argue that all the Chinese and Thai and Italian restaurants in America show that the United States is losing its distinctive character.

Have France, Germany, and Italy lost their distinctive qualities? Have any countries? On the basis of my travels, I would suggest that the monoculture hypothesis is a generalization that cannot be supported; that it is only true in a very superficial manner, if that. The Lévi-Strauss monoculture hypothesis is a generalization, like those of Daniel Boorstin, written from an elitist perspective and lacking any empirical basis of support. Maybe the world is becoming that contradiction in terms, a multicultural monoculture, or monoculturally multicultural, but I tend to doubt that such is the case.

Thailand Tourism
© 2007 by The Haworth Press, Inc. All rights reserved.
doi:10.1300/5789_08

Thailand, I submit, is a wonderful example of the way countries can modernize without throwing out the baby of a distinctive and interesting culture with the bath water of modernization and so-called progress. The very architecture of Thailand suggests that the mono-culture hypothesis is overdrawn. The fantastic *wats,* with their Bud-dhas and stupas, refute the monoculture hypothesis. And so do the monks in their saffron robes.

In their *Footprint Thailand Handbook,* Joshua Eliot and Jane Bikersteth offer a capsule description of Thailand as a tourist cliché. They write:

> Thailand is an Asian cliché. Exotic, inscrutable, hot, Oriental, delicate, sumptuous. Take the first few hours of an average visi-tor's arrival in Bangkok. Off the plane and into a gleaming new airport terminal. Lilting Thai voices and a strange alphabet. Into the city along an elevated highway in the company of an appar-ently deranged taxi driver, with a magic diagram inscribed on the roof of his car, a picture of a long-dead king lodged rever-ently in the tachometer, a cheap gold Buddha glued to the top of the dashboard and a garland of plastic frangipangi hanging from the rear-view mirror. Out of the taxi and into a quiet, cool hotel with copies of the Asian Wall Street Journal artfully arranged on reception and CNN in the bedrooms. Or into a small guesthouse run by a Thai bobbing to Bob Marley and offering sweltering rooms the size of chicken coops for the price of a dozen eggs. (2003: 12)

This passage captures the kind of shock that travelers might experi-ence when they arrive in Thailand and describes the interesting com-bination of what we might call the Thai sensibility and Western pop culture that one finds in Thailand. How important is this popular cul-ture and what effects might it be having? That is a question that Ian Buruma deals with in his analysis of Thai identity.

IAN BURUMA ON THAI IDENTITY

One problem that scholarly studies of tourism continually deal with involves the matter of whether tourism has powerful and lasting impacts upon the identities of the countries where it flourishes. There are, of course, obvious impacts: hotels are built, roads are built, a tourist infrastructure develops, and cities and other areas become increasingly dependent upon tourist expenditures.

Some tourism scholars argue that tourism is a kind of soft colonialism, and that it has profound effects upon the countries where it becomes a major source of revenue. Since tourism is a global phenomenon, it is suggested that the world is losing its variety and, as discussed earlier, it is becoming a monoculture. And Thailand, since it is so dependent upon tourism, might be a good example of how Thai identity has been shaped by tourism—especially tourism from first-world countries. I would argue that tourism does have an impact on all societies, but generally speaking it has a superficial impact that is not long-lasting, as Thais adapt certain aspects of Western society, whether it be fast-food joints or clothing and integrate them into their own culture.

There is support for this argument. In his book *God's Dust: A Modern Asian Journey,* Ian Buruma argues that the Thais have been able to maintain their cultural identity, even if there is a patina of Westernization that is to be found in various places in the country. He writes:

> It is easy for the visitor to Bangkok to feel that he is in a fake world, a world of images, of empty forms, foreign styles divorced from any meaning. It is easy to condemn Thailand, or at least Bangkok, for being so hopelessly corrupted by "Westernization," "cultural imperialism," "Coca-Colonization," or whatever one wants to call it, that it has lost its identity altogether; indeed, a place where people fool themselves for fun. . . . Under the evanescent surface, Thais remain in control of themselves. Perhaps because of this shimmering, ever-changing, ever-so-thin surface, Thailand, to me, is one of the most elusive countries in Asia. Thais clearly do not suffer from the colonial hang-ups of neighboring peoples; they know who they are. And yet trying to grasp or even touch the essence of Thailand seems impossible, like pinning down water. (Quoted in O'Reilly and Habegger, eds., 2002: 367)

This elusive quality is, I think, one of the things that fascinates tourists (*farangs,* as the Thais put it) about the country. When you travel there you sense that there is something interesting about the country, but it is hard to put your finger on it. What is interesting is the way the Thais have both adopted certain Western ways and maintained their cultural identity.

Buruma quotes a Thai architect, Sumet Jumsai:

> We seem to take over only the veneer of other cultures . . . but our essence is still there, like the wooden houses behind the modern department stores. Opposites always coexist in Thailand. (Quoted in O'Reilly and Habegger, eds., 2002: 369)

That seems to be at the heart of the Thai enigma—opposites coexisting when, to the Western mind, they should not and cannot do so, just as opposite flavors in Thai food coexist, yielding taste sensations quite foreign to visitors. The Thais seem to have a unique ability to take up things, like Westernization, and then discard them, when they are tired of them or when they are no longer useful.

There are oppositions to be found in all cultures. Cultures seem to carry on dialogues with themselves over the years. But usually, it is one side of the pair of opposites that dominates. So a culture in which both oppositions coexist, if Buruma is correct, is quite enigmatic to visitors to Thailand. Aristotle taught that something cannot be "A" and "not A" at the same time, but that seems to be what Thailand is all about.

THE TOURIST AS AMATEUR ANTHROPOLOGIST

In his classic work, *Argonauts of the Western Pacific,* anthropologist Bronislaw Malinowski suggested that the task of the anthropologist, when studying primitive cultures, is to investigate in a scientific manner what he described as the "imponderabilia" of everyday life. He writes:

> There is a series of phenomena of great importance which cannot possibly be recorded by questioning or computing documents, but have to be observed in their full actuality. Let us call

them the imponderabilia of actual life. Here belong such things as the routine of a man's working day, the details of his care of the body, of the manner of taking food and preparing it; the tone of conversational and social life around the village fires, the existence of strong friendships or hostilities, and of passing sympathies and dislikes between people; the subtle yet unmistakable manner in which personal vanities and ambitions are reflected in the behaviour of the individual and in the emotional reactions of those who surround him. All these facts can and ought to be scientifically formulated and recorded, but it is necessary that this be done, not by a superficial registration of details, as is usually done by untrained observers, but with an effort at penetrating the mental attitude expressed in them. (1961: 18-19)

This is the world to which the tourist is exposed—the world of everyday life—and it is the quality of everyday life in the countries that tourists visit that is of importance to them. The tourist may be an "untrained observer," as Malinowski put it, but even untrained observers are able to notice how people dress, how they relate to one another, the way they dress, the way they *wai* one another, and things like that. And tourists are able to visit their sacred places (there are something like 300 *wats* in Bangkok) and sample the foods that people in other cultures eat.

THAILAND AS A TEXT

Thus Thailand presents itself to tourists, whatever their particular interests as tourists (ecotourists, sex tourists, culture tourists), as a culture to be studied and understood and lived in, and one in which the mental attitudes of the Thais, their psyches, present themselves as enigmas and puzzlements to be understood. There is a vast difference between learning about a country such as Thailand in guidebooks, in reading about it in travel books, and actually being in the country.

And the signs, by which we interpret Thailand, can be deceiving. For example, the "long-neck women" in the Padaung refugee villages seem to have unnaturally extended necks, thanks to the brass ornaments that the Padaung women wear around their necks. When you look at these women, it seems as if they have separate brass circles around their necks; but in reality, they are all part of a long coil that Padaung women (and their daughters) wear, and take off at times. As Joe Cummings explains in the 2003 edition of the *Lonely Planet Thailand,* in actuality what happens is that these coils (which generally weigh around five kilograms) depress their collarbones and their rib cages, making it look like their necks are unusually long.

This example suggests that we have to be extremely careful in the way we analyze Thai culture and, in particular, signifiers of Thailand, because, as the Padaung women show us, our eyes can deceive us. And Thailand, because of the particular nature of its culture and various subcultures, because of the Thais' politeness and desire to please, can easily deceive us.

You can describe Thailand (or any country) endlessly, but these descriptions can take a person only so far, and actually being in a country and interacting with the people provides something no descriptions can capture. No matter how insulated tourists may be in their "bubbles" (five-star hotels that are international in nature), they have to walk around, see how buildings are designed and what street life is, and they observe the "imponderabilia" that Malinowski wrote about.

It was this imponderabilia that interested me in Thailand—the basic aspects of Thai life, the things you see when you walk around, the "significant trivia" that make up life there, and I took it upon myself to interpret these phenomena as best I could.

For me, Thailand was a text. (I use "text" as it is used in academic discourse to describe a novel, a story, a symphony or opera, an advertisement, etc.) I tried, as best I could, to interpret this text, understand the roles of the main characters in this text, and to explain its most salient features while, at the same time, showing how tourism has informed this text as a dominant theme. My plot, so to speak, was everyday life and the dominant theme was tourism. Tourism is the biggest industry in Thailand and, as such, it has played an important role in shaping, and in some cases preserving, certain aspects of Thai society, culture, and everyday life there. Thais recognize that if they are not careful and do not maintain their ancient sites, their beautiful beaches, their ethnic and cultural diversity, and natural areas where too much traffic could be destructive, their success as a tourist destination could destroy what it is that tourists seek in Thailand.

THAILAND AND THE HUMAN SPIRIT

There is much to be gained, I would suggest, from spending time in a country like Thailand. It is a strikingly beautiful country and its beauty has a salutary effect on us the same way that listening to beautiful music or seeing beautiful works of art or eating a wonderful meal with friends helps uplift our spirits and does something for our souls.

In her book *Materializing Thailand,* Penny Van Esterik makes an important point about the power of beauty and of aesthetics. She writes:

> Attraction to Thailand is partly aesthetic—the beauty of the country's natural and constructed environments; the Thai enjoyment of things beautiful—orchids, textiles, temples, people; the civility and grace of its peoples; their appreciation of the present moment, and the ease with which the ugly and painful is slipped out of sight. Only within the ascetic system of Theravada Buddhism is sensual pleasure denied, drawing even more attention to the beauty of ascetic simplicity made more striking beside baroque extravagance. Even the dramatic contrasts between wealth and poverty, between Buddhist denial and total indulgence, fascinate rather than repulse. There are no rewards for suppressing beauty or pleasure. This has been in the past and continues to be the fascination of Thailand for travellers and analysts alike. (2000: 3)

The Thais trade on the beauty of the country, the beauty of their women, the baroque splendor of their *wats,* and the many sites of historical interest that exist in the country. And, as Van Esterik explains, the Thais have done an excellent job of making aspects of their royal court culture available to tourists, as well. The Thais have, she suggests, commodified their culture and traditions for tourists, but they have also been very careful to maintain them. There had been a movement to develop a pan-Thai national culture in the 1940s and to destroy regional cultures, but this failed and, ironically, she adds, as a result of tourism, many regional traditions have been reborn and reinvigorated. She quotes a Thai writer, Sujit Wongtet who wrote in

The Bangkok Post (September 5, 1990), "If we are confident in our own culture, there is no need to be afraid of tourism" (2002: 120).

Ten million foreign tourists visit Thailand every year. In 2005, 12 million tourists were expected, although the tsunami that wreaked such havoc on Thailand (and many other countries as well) may have affected that number. They come, as I have suggested earlier, for many different reasons. But there is a common thread behind all these visits—and that is Thai culture, a rich, complex, and fascinating one that tourists experience from the moment they set foot in Bangkok or wherever. Thailand is a country that has the power to transform us, to enhance our sense of possibility, to enlarge our understanding of human beings and spending time in this beautiful country, with its refined cuisine, its fascinating culture, its lovely beaches, its kindly and spirited people, is, for most tourists I would suggest, a spiritually enriching experience, and for some, a truly profound experience.

Tourists spend time in a country. They spend, on average, a bit more than a week in Thailand. And when they leave, they find that, magically, some of Thailand remains in them—in their memories of their experiences there, in their remembrances of the sights they saw, in their recollections of their adventures, and, most of all, in their hearts and in their sense of possibility.

References

Barnouw, Victor (1973). *Culture and Personality.* Homewood, IL: Dorsey.
Barthes, Roland (1975). *The Pleasure of the Text.* New York: Hill and Wang.
—— (1982). *Empire of Signs.* New York: Hill and Wang.
Baudrillard, Jean (1998). *The Consumer Society: Myths and Structures.* London: Sage Publications.
Berger, Arthur Asa (2003). *Media and Society: A Critical Perspective.* Lanham, MD: Rowman and Littlefield Publishers, Inc.
—— (2004). *Deconstructing Travel: Cultural Perspectives on Tourism.* Walnut Creek, CA: AltaMira Press.
—— (2005). *Media Analysis Techniques,* Third Edition. Thousand Oaks: Sage Publications.
—— (2005). *Vietnam Tourism.* Binghamton, NY: The Haworth Hospitality Press.
Boorstin, Daniel J. (1975). *The Image: A Guide to Pseudo-Events in America.* New York: Athaneum.
Brown, Patricia L. (1993). In the City of Change, Is "Las Vegas Landmark" an Oxymoron? *The New York Times,* October 7: A13.
Burns, Jim (Ed.) (1991). *Gault Millau: The Best of Thailand.* New York: Prentice Hall.
Buruma, Ian (1989). *God's Dust: A Modern Asian Journey.* New York: Farrar, Straus and Giroux.
Certeau, Michel de (1984). *The Practice of Everyday Life.* Berkeley: University of California Press.
Cohen, Erik (1996). *Thai Tourism: Hill Tribes, Islands and Open-Ended Prostitution.* Bangkok: White Lotus.
—— (2000). *The Commercialized Crafts of Thailand: Hill Tribes and Lowland Villages.* Honolulu: University of Hawaii Press.
Cornwel-Smith, Philip (2005). *Very Thai: Everyday Popular Culture.* Bangkok: River Books.
Cummings, Joe (1990). *Thailand,* Fourth Edition. Hawthorn, AU: Lonely Planet Publications.
——, Sandra Bao, Steven Martin, and China Williams (2003). *Thailand,* Tenth Edition. Melbourne, AU: Lonely Planet Publications.
Durkheim, Emile (1965).*The Elementary Forms of Religious Life.* New York: Free Press.

Thailand Tourism
© 2007 by The Haworth Press, Inc. All rights reserved.
doi:10.1300/5789_09

Eliade, Mircea (1961). *The Sacred and the Profane: The Nature of Religion.* New York: Harper and Row.

Eliot, Joshua and Jane Bickersteth (2003). *Footprint Thailand Handbook,* Fourth Edition. Bath, UK: Footprint Handbooks.

Florence, Mason and Robert Storey (1999). *Vietnam,* Fifth Edition. Melbourne, AU: Lonely Planet Publications.

Frisby, David and Mike Featherstone (Eds.) (1997). *Simmel on Culture.* London: Sage Publications.

Fussell, Paul (Ed.) (1987). *The Norton Book of Travel.* New York: Norton.

Gray, Paul and Lucy Ridout (1992). *Rough Guide to Thailand.* New York: Prentice Hall Travel.

Gunther, John (1939). *Inside Asia.* New York: Harper and Brothers.

Holmes, Henry and Suchanon Tangtongtavy (1997). *Working with the Thais: A Guide to Managing in Thailand.* Bangkok: White Lotus.

Honko, Lauri (Ed.) (1972). *Science of Religion Studies in Methodology.* The Hague, the Netherlands: Mouton.

Iyer, Pico (1989). *Video Night in Katmandu.* New York: Vintage. (Quoted in James O'Reilly and Larry Habegger, eds., *Travelers' Tales Thailand,* 2002: 20.)

Kulick, Eliott and Dick Wilson (1992). *Thailand's Turn: Profile of a New Dragon.* New York: St. Martin's Press.

Lakoff, George and Mark Johnson (1980). *Metaphors We Live By.* Chicago: University of Chicago Press.

Lander, Nicholas (2004). Wok You see is What You Get. *Financial Times.* December 11.

Leed, Eric J. (1991). *The Mind of the Traveler: From Gilgamesh to Global Tourism.* New York: Basic Books.

Lefebvre, Henri (1971). *Everyday Life in the Modern World.* New York: Harper and Row.

Lévi-Strauss, Claude (1970). *Tristes Tropiques: An Anthropological Study of Primitive Societies in Brazil.* New York: Athaneum.

MacCannell, Dean (1976). *The Tourist: A New Theory of the Leisure Class.* New York: Schocken.

Malinowski, Bronislaw (1961). *Argonauts of the Western Pacific.* New York: Dutton.

Marshall, Andrew (2005). The Thais that bind. *Time: Asia.* March 14: 47.

Matzner, Andrew (2000). Not a Pretty Picture: Images of Married Life in Thai Comic Books. *International Journal of Comic Art* 2(1): 57-75.

O'Reilly, James and Larry Habegger (eds.) (2002). *Travelers' Tales: Thailand.* San Francisco: Travelers' Tales.

Pratt, Mary Louise (1992). *Imperial Eyes: Travel Writing and Transculturatation.* London: Routledge.

Saussure, Ferdinand de (1966). *A Course in General Linguistics.* New York: McGraw-Hill.

Seabrook, Jeremy (2001). *Travels in the Skin Trade: Tourism and the Sex Industry.* London: Pluto Press.

Spiro, Melford E. (1979). Symbolism and Functionalism in the Anthropological Study of Religion. In Lauri Honko (Ed.), *Science of Religion: Studies in Methodology*. The Hague, the Netherlands: Mouton.

Tambiah, S. J. (1973). Classification of Animals in Thailand. In Mary Douglas (Ed.), *Rules and Meanings*, 127-166. Harmondsworth, UK: Penguin.

Toews, Bea and Robert McGregor (1998). *Culture Shock: Succeed in Business Thailand*. Portland, OR: Graphic Arts Center Publishing.

Urry, John. Globalizing the Tourist Gaze. *The Tourist Gaze.* Lancaster: University of Lancaster Press. http://www.comp.lancs.ac.uk/sociology/soc079ju.html.

Van Esteric, Penny (2000). *Materializing Thailand*. Oxford: Berg.

Wikipedia. (2004). Tourism. Available at http://en.wikipedia.org/wiki/Tourism. Accessed November 14.

World Tourism Organization (2002a). Statistics. Available at: http://www.world tourism.org. Accessed May 15.

World Tourism Organization (2002b). World's Top 15 Tourism Destinations. Available at: http://www.world-tourism.org.

World Tourism Organization (2004). Newsroom. Available at: http://www.world tourism.org. Accessed November 14.

Wyatt, David K. (1984). *Thailand: A Short History*. New Haven, CT: Yale University Press.

Index

Page numbers followed by the letter "t" indicate tables.

Thailand Tourism
© 2007 by The Haworth Press, Inc. All rights reserved.
doi:10.1300/5789_10

THE HAWORTH HOSPITALITY & TOURISM PRESS™
Hospitality, Travel, and Tourism
K. S. Chon, PhD, Editor in Chief

THAILAND TOURISM by Arthur Asa Berger. (2007).

CULTURAL TOURISM: GLOBAL AND LOCAL PERSPECTIVES edited by Greg Richards. (2007). "An excellent collection of material that builds upon the editor's previous studies in the field as well as the work of ATLAS. Not only does the book reflect extremely well on the high quality of work that comes out of the ATLAS network on cultural tourism, but the work further reinforces Greg Richards' profile as a leader in the cultural tourism field." *C. Michael Hall, BA (Hons), MA, PhD, Professor, Department of Tourism, University of Otago*

GAY TOURISM: CULTURE AND CONTEXT by Gordon Waitt and Kevin Markwell. (2006). "This book provides an international overview of gay destinations and spaces. It addresses issues of how the tourism industry, in its search for the 'pink dollar,' yet again seeks to commodify and normalize experiences within commercial settings, and thus creates stereotypes that are not wholly satisfying for gay men. The authors are not afraid to court controversy by addressing gay issues in Islamic societies. In short, there is much in this book for tourism researchers unfamiliar with the social context of gay tourism. Such readers will emerge both better informed and with further questions to prompt their own thinking." *Chris Ryan, PhD, Professor of Tourism, University of Waikato Management School, New Zealand*

CASES IN SUSTAINABLE TOURISM: AN EXPERIENTIAL APPROACH TO MAKING DECISIONS edited by Irene M. Herremans. (2006). "As a tourism instructor and researcher, I recommend this textbook for both undergraduate and graduate students who wish to pursue their careers in parks, recreation, or tourism. The text is appropriate both for junior and senior tourism management classes and graduate classes. It is an excellent primer for understanding the fundamental concepts, issues, and real-world examples of sustainable tourism." *Hwan-Suk Chris Choi, PhD, Assistant Professor, School of Hospitality and Tourism Management, University of Guelph*

COMMUNITY DESTINATION MANAGEMENT IN DEVELOPING ECONOMIES edited by Walter Jamieson. (2006). "This book is a welcome and valuable addition to the destination management literature, focusing as it does on developing economies in the Asian context. It provides an unusually comprehensive and informative overview of critical issues in the field, effectively combining well-crafted discussions of key conceptual and methodological issues with carefully selected and well-presented case studies drawn from a number of contrasting Asian destinations." *Peter Hills, PhD, Professor and Director, The Centre of Urban Planning and Environmental Management, The University of Hong Kong*

MANAGING SUSTAINABLE TOURISM: A LEGACY FOR THE FUTURE by David L. Edgell Sr. (2006). "This comprehensive book on sustainable tourism should be required reading for everyone interested in tourism. The author is masterful in defining strategies and using case studies to explain best practices in generating long-term economic return on your tourism investment." *Kurtis M. Ruf, Partner, Ruf Strategic Solutions; Author,* Contemporary Database Marketing

CASINO INDUSTRY IN ASIA PACIFIC: DEVELOPMENT, OPERATION, AND IMPACT edited by Cathy H.C. Hsu. (2006). "This book is a must-read for anyone interested in the opportunities and challenges that the proliferation of casino gaming will bring to Asia in the early twenty-first century. The economic and social consequences of casino gaming in Asia may ultimately prove to be far more significant than those encountered in the West, and this book opens the door as to what those consequences might be." *William R. Eadington, PhD, Professor of Economics and Director, Institute for the Study of Gambling and Commercial Gaming, University of Nevada, Reno*

THE GROWTH STRATEGIES OF HOTEL CHAINS: BEST BUSINESS PRACTICES BY LEADING COMPANIES by Onofre Martorell Cunill. (2006). "Informative, well-written, and up-to-date. This is one title that I shall certainly be adding to my 'must-read' list for students this year." *Tom Baum, PhD, Professor of International Tourism and Hospitality Management, The Scottish Hotel School, The University of Strathclyde, Glasgow*

HANDBOOK FOR DISTANCE LEARNING IN TOURISM by Gary Williams. (2005). "This is an important book for a variety of audiences. As a resource for educational designers (and their managers) in particular, it is invaluable. The book is easy to read, and is full of practical information that can be logically applied in the design and development of flexible learning resources." *Louise Berg, MA, DipED, Lecturer in Education, Charles Sturt University, Australia*

VIETNAM TOURISM by Arthur Asa Berger. (2005). "Fresh and innovative.... Drawing upon Professor Berger's background and experience in cultural studies, this book offers an imaginative and personal portrayal of Vietnam as a tourism destination.... A very welcome addition to the field of destination studies." *Professor Brian King, PhD, Head, School of Hospitality, Tourism & Marketing, Victoria University, Australia*

TOURISM AND HOTEL DEVELOPMENT IN CHINA: FROM POLITICAL TO ECONOMIC SUCCESS by Hanqin Qiu Zhang, Ray Pine, and Terry Lam. (2005). "This is one of the most comprehensive books on China tourism and hotel development. It is one of the best textbooks for educators, students, practitioners, and investors who are interested in China tourism and hotel industry. Readers will experience vast, diversified, and past and current issues that affect every educator, student, practitioner, and investor in China tourism and hotel globally in an instant." *Hailin Qu, PhD, Full Professor and William E. Davis Distinguished Chair, School of Hotel & Restaurant Administration, Oklahoma State University*

THE TOURISM AND LEISURE INDUSTRY: SHAPING THE FUTURE edited by Klaus Weiermair and Christine Mathies. (2004). "If you need or want to know about the impact of globalization, the impact of technology, societal forces of change, the experience economy, adaptive technologies, environmental changes, or the new trend of slow tourism, you need this book. *The Tourism and Leisure Industry* contains a great mix of research and practical information." *Charles R. Goeldner, PhD, Professor Emeritus of Marketing and Tourism, Leeds School of Business, University of Colorado*

OCEAN TRAVEL AND CRUISING: A CULTURAL ANALYSIS by Arthur Asa Berger. (2004). "Dr. Berger presents an interdisciplinary discussion of the cruise industry for the thinking person. This is an enjoyable social psychology travel guide with a little business management thrown in. A great book for the curious to read a week before embarking on a first cruise or for the frequent cruiser to gain a broader insight into exactly what a cruise experience represents." *Carl Braunlich, DBA, Associate Professor, Department of Hospitality and Tourism Management, Purdue University, West Lafayette, Indiana*

STANDING THE HEAT: ENSURING CURRICULUM QUALITY IN CULINARY ARTS AND GASTRONOMY by Joseph A. Hegarty. (2003). "This text provides the genesis of a well-researched, thoughtful, rigorous, and sound theoretical framework for the enlargement and expansion of higher education programs in culinary arts and gastronomy." *John M. Antun, PhD, Founding Director, National Restaurant Institute, School of Hotel, Restaurant, and Tourism Management, University of South Carolina*

SEX AND TOURISM: JOURNEYS OF ROMANCE, LOVE, AND LUST edited by Thomas G. Bauer and Bob McKercher. (2003). "Anyone interested in or concerned about the impact of tourism on society and particularly in the developing world, should read this book. It explores a subject that has long remained ignored, almost a taboo area for many governments, institutions, and organizations. It demonstrates that the stereotyping of 'sex tourism' is too simple and travel and sex have many manifestations. The book follows its theme in an innovative and original way." *Carson L. Jenkins, PhD, Professor of International Tourism, University of Strathclyde, Glasgow, Scotland*

CONVENTION TOURISM: INTERNATIONAL RESEARCH AND INDUSTRY PERSPECTIVES edited by Karin Weber and Kye-Sung Chon. (2002). "This comprehensive book is truly global in its perspective. The text points out areas of needed research—a great starting point for graduate students, university faculty, and industry professionals alike. While the focus is mainly academic, there is a lot of meat for this burgeoning industry to chew on as well." *Patti J. Shock, CPCE, Professor and Department Chair, Tourism and Convention Administration, Harrah College of Hotel Administration, University of Nevada–Las Vegas*

CULTURAL TOURISM: THE PARTNERSHIP BETWEEN TOURISM AND CULTURAL HERITAGE MANAGEMENT by Bob McKercher and Hilary du Cros. (2002). "The book brings together concepts, perspectives, and practicalities that must be understood by both cultural heritage and tourism managers, and as such is a must-read for both." *Hisashi B. Sugaya, AICP, Former Chair, International Council of Monuments and Sites, International Scientific Committee on Cultural Tourism; Former Executive Director, Pacific Asia Travel Association Foundation, San Francisco, CA*

TOURISM IN THE ANTARCTIC: OPPORTUNITIES, CONSTRAINTS, AND FUTURE PROSPECTS by Thomas G. Bauer. (2001). "Thomas Bauer presents a wealth of detailed information on the challenges and opportunities facing tourism operators in this last great tourism frontier." *David Mercer, PhD, Associate Professor, School of Geography & Environmental Science, Monash University, Melbourne, Australia*

SERVICE QUALITY MANAGEMENT IN HOSPITALITY, TOURISM, AND LEISURE edited by Jay Kandampully, Connie Mok, and Beverley Sparks. (2001). "A must-read. . . . a treasure. . . . pulls together the work of scholars across the globe, giving you access to new ideas, international research, and industry examples from around the world." *John Bowen, Professor and Director of Graduate Studies, William F. Harrah College of Hotel Administration, University of Nevada, Las Vegas*

TOURISM IN SOUTHEAST ASIA: A NEW DIRECTION edited by K. S. (Kaye) Chon. (2000). "Presents a wide array of very topical discussions on the specific challenges facing the tourism industry in Southeast Asia. A great resource for both scholars and practitioners." *Dr. Hubert B. Van Hoof, Assistant Dean/Associate Professor, School of Hotel and Restaurant Management, Northern Arizona University*

THE PRACTICE OF GRADUATE RESEARCH IN HOSPITALITY AND TOURISM edited by K. S. Chon. (1999). "An excellent reference source for students pursuing graduate degrees in hospitality and tourism." *Connie Mok, PhD, CHE, Associate Professor, Conrad N. Hilton College of Hotel and Restaurant Management, University of Houston, Texas*

THE INTERNATIONAL HOSPITALITY MANAGEMENT BUSINESS: MANAGEMENT AND OPERATIONS by Larry Yu. (1999). "The abundant real-world examples and cases provided in the text enable readers to understand the most up-to-date developments in international hospitality business." *Zheng Gu, PhD, Associate Professor, College of Hotel Administration, University of Nevada, Las Vegas*

CONSUMER BEHAVIOR IN TRAVEL AND TOURISM by Abraham Pizam and Yoel Mansfeld. (1999). "A must for anyone who wants to take advantage of new global opportunities in this growing industry." *Bonnie J. Knutson, PhD, School of Hospitality Business, Michigan State University*

LEGALIZED CASINO GAMING IN THE UNITED STATES: THE ECONOMIC AND SOCIAL IMPACT edited by Cathy H. C. Hsu. (1999). "Brings a fresh new look at one of the areas in tourism that has not yet received careful and serious consideration in the past." *Muzaffer Uysal, PhD, Professor of Tourism Research, Virginia Polytechnic Institute and State University, Blacksburg*

HOSPITALITY MANAGEMENT EDUCATION edited by Clayton W. Barrows and Robert H. Bosselman. (1999). "Takes the mystery out of how hospitality management education programs function and serves as an excellent resource for individuals interested in pursuing the field." *Joe Perdue, CCM, CHE, Director, Executive Masters Program, College of Hotel Administration, University of Nevada, Las Vegas*

MARKETING YOUR CITY, U.S.A.: A GUIDE TO DEVELOPING A STRATEGIC TOURISM MARKETING PLAN by Ronald A. Nykiel and Elizabeth Jascolt. (1998). "An excellent guide for anyone involved in the planning and marketing of cities and regions. . . . A terrific job of synthesizing an otherwise complex procedure." *James C. Maken, PhD, Associate Professor, Babcock Graduate School of Management, Wake Forest University, Winston-Salem, North Carolina*

For Product Safety Concerns and Information please contact our EU representative GPSR@taylorandfrancis.com Taylor & Francis Verlag GmbH, Kaufingerstraße 24, 80331 München, Germany

Printed and bound by CPI Group (UK) Ltd, Croydon, CR0 4YY

08/05/2025

01864553-0001